# Today Is
# *Mine*

# Today Is
## *Mine*

The Holy Bible, New King James Version (NKJV) Copyright © 1982
by Thomas Nelson, Inc. Used by permission.
January 2, 8, 9, 11, 15-18, 20-24, 26-30
February 3, 4, 6, 7, 9, 11-13, 15-19, 21, 22, 24, 26-28
March 1, 4, 8-11, 14, 16, 18-20, 22, 24-28, 30
April 1-5, 7, 8, 10, 11, 13-18, 20, 23-25, 27-29
May 1-3, 5-8, 12, 15-18, 20-25, 30, 31
June 4-12, 14, 15-25, 27-30,
July 2-6, 8, 10-13, 15-17, 20, 21, 23, 24, 26-31
August 1-5, 7, 9-31
September 4-10, 14, 15, 18-24, 26, 28, 30
October 1-4, 7, 9, 12-16, 18-23, 26, 27, 30, 31
November 5-8, 10, 15, 17, 18, 21, 22, 26, 27, 29, 30

HOLY BIBLE, NEW INTERNATIONAL VERSION (NIV) Copyright © 1973,
1978, 1984 by International Bible Society, Used by permission.
June 13; July 1, 14, 19
August 6, 8
September 2, 11, 16
October 5, 8, 11, 17, 29,
December 3, 4, 9, 10, 12, 14, 17, 18, 21, 28, 31

All other Scripture references are from the King James Version or are
author's paraphrase.

Brownlow Publishing Company, Inc.
6309 Airport Freeway, Fort Worth, Texas 76117

*This Book Belongs To*

_____

_____

_____

# Today Is
# *Mine*

*365 original daily devotions,*

*inspirational quotes, and*

*thought-provoking Scriptures*

*for mastering the art of living.*

# Leroy Brownlow

*Brownlow*

**BROWNLOW PUBLISHING COMPANY, INC.**

# EDITOR'S PREFACE

In 1972, a gifted young minister (my Dad) was asked by a prominent publisher to write a daily devotional book. He wrote the book, working late at night and early mornings, but decided to publish it himself. He called it <u>Today Is Mine</u>. Since then, it has sold over a half million copies and blessed countless lives.

The book has a simple formula:
- A short, original essay by the author, brief and to the point,
- A related quotation from a well known literary source,
- A brief Scripture reference on the topic thus confirming the Bible's relevance to everyday life.

The book was an instant success and became a classic. It is our honor and privilege to publish this new edition.

PAUL C. BROWNLOW

# FOREWORD

*H*erein is my philosophy, presented in 365 brief essays, expressed in simple language, supported by the cherished words of the most renowned authors, philosophers, scholars and statesmen of all ages, plus quotations from the Bible.

It is obvious from the many quotations which bear on the topics that this volume is more than one man's view of life, that it is actually the tried and tested views of man through the centuries; and this is not surprising, for the true principles of successful living are not new. As Cicero said, "Nothing quite new is perfect." Truth is always truth, no matter when and how and by whom it is expressed.

It is my belief that these basic principles of life will help to give each day to the person who ponders them; and just as these reflections have pointed and inspired me to happier and fuller days, the hope is now entertained that they will help others.

LEROY BROWNLOW

# RESOLUTIONS

*I* am resolved:

- To forget past mistakes and press on to greater achievements
- To put first things first
- To make my work a joy.
- To allow nothing to disturb my peace of mind
- To never lose self-control
- To spend so much time improving myself that I have no time for criticism of others
- To think the best, work for it and expect it
- To be a friend to all
- To stand for the right
- To be true
- To be kind
- To take every disappointment as a stimulant
- To live on the sunny side of every cloud
- To smile
- To look ahead
- To keep moving

*Resolve to perform what you ought; perform without fail what you resolve.*

— Benjamin Franklin
1706-1790

*I am resolved what to do.*

— Luke 16:4

*January 2*

# PRAYER AT THE NEW YEAR

*And* these thoughts I pray:

May I make every day mine, not waste a one; look forward, not backward. Grant me a life of peace, free from strife, animosity, resentment and retaliation. Help me to be a friend to all people, even to those who dislike me, manifesting more tolerance. May I be quick to see my own faults, and even quicker to correct them. Endue me with a gentle, kind and helpful spirit. May I abhor the evil, cleave to the good. Give me strength to be genuine. Help me to count the cost and to pay the fare. May I walk with Thee— unto the end!

*'Tis Heaven alone that is given away;*
*'Tis only God may be had for the asking.*
— James Russell Lowell
1819 -1891

*Therefore Your servant found it in his heart to pray this*
*prayer to You.*
— II Samuel 7:27

## January 3

# BEGIN THE PORTRAIT NOW

After a silver-haired visitor with mellow manners had left the home of friends, a young daughter, greatly impressed, commented to her mother: "Oh, if I could be an old lady like that, so sweet, serene, lovable and beautiful, I wouldn't mind being old."

The brilliant and discerning mother replied: "Remember— that kind of a spirit was not grown in a hurry. It took her a long time to become what she is. And if you are going to be that kind of an old lady, if you are going to paint yourself to be a portrait like that, you had better start mixing the colors and brushing a few strokes now."

*Progress, man's distinctive mark alone,*
*Not God's, and not the beasts': God is, they are;*
*Man partly is, and wholly hopes to be.*
— Robert Browning
1812-1889

*Let us go on unto perfection.*
— Hebrews 6:1

*January 4*

## WE MAKE OUR OWN WORLD

The world is a lot of things to a lot of people: generally, what each makes it, a beautiful and beneficial world to those who dig out its beauty and blessings. The good find good, and the evil find evil. For, in the last analysis, the world is a mirror which reflects the little world each is.

There may be such a thing as good luck, but only in sparing uncertainties. The more certain rule is: God blesses him who blesses himself. The tree grows the lumber, but not the house. Food feeds the body, but doesn't make the person; that we must do for ourselves with God's help.

*No man ever wetted clay and then left it,*
*as if there would be bricks by chance and fortune.*
— Plutarch
46-120

*Whoso is wise, and will observe these things, even they shall*
*understand the loving-kindness of the Lord.*
— Psalm 107:43

# YOU— NOT YOUR ANCESTORS

*Y*ou are neither a born winner nor a born loser. The way you play the game determines that.

It's our general behavior— not our genealogy— that makes the difference. It's not the blue blood our parents gave us— but the dogged effort we give that runs up the score. It's not who our forefathers were— but what we are— that makes the difference.

This generation will not let us hang onto our ancestors' coat tails; neither will it deny us a coat because they didn't have one. But we will have to earn it.

*They will ask you, "What have you done?*
*Not, "Who are your ancestors?"*
*The famous veil in the sanctuary*
*Is not reverenced by the faithful*
*Because it came from the silkworm.*

— Saasi, the Persian poet

*The son shall not bear the iniquity of the father, neither shall*
*the father bear the iniquity of the son: the righteousness of*
*the righteous shall be upon him, and the wickedness of the*
*wicked shall be upon him.*

— Ezekiel 18:20

# JUST FOR TODAY

In a McGuffey's Reader there is a story of an old clock that suddenly quit running. The reason: the clock counted the number of times it would have to tick in one year— 31,536,000 times. This was just too many ticks for a weary clock; so it lost its morale and stopped. Later it was explained to the clock all that was expected of it was to tick just one tick at a time. With this reflection, it regained its spirit and began running again.

So it is with us. Trying to live life all in a lump is frightening. All that is necessary is to do our duty and give our best today.

*He who governed the world before I was born shall take care of it likewise when I am dead. My part is to improve the present moment.*
— John Wesley
1703-1791

*They shall run, and not be weary; and they shall walk, and not faint.*
— Isaiah 40:31

## AN IDEAL GOAL

*E*ach person should have this goal: May I become wiser, better and happier. All other earthly accomplishments are empty and vain. No matter what we have acquired— wealth, education, prestige— we must ask ourselves: Are we wiser? Are we better? Are we happier?

If not, we must look for the cause in our own hearts. Probably we will find that we need to develop more self-control and less irritation; more deliberation and less impulsiveness; more faith and less doubt. It is largely an internal problem. For out of the heart are the issues of life.

*It is only with the heart that one can see rightly; what is essential is invisible to the eye.*
— Antoine de Saint-Exupéry
1900-1944

*I thought on my ways, and turned my feet unto thy testimonies.*
— Psalm 119:59

# THOUGH WE BEGIN SMALL

Fret not at small beginnings. The oak began as an acorn. The beautiful rainbow had its beginning in a drop of rain and a ray of light. The oozing through of one drop of water started the proverbial break in the dike. The muscular athlete once had trouble crawling. The university graduate started in the first grade. The massive international oil industry began with a little shallow well. Today's aviation can be traced back to a most humble beginning. A cent is the beginning of a dollar— ninety-nine more to go; it's little and cheap, but very religious— goes to church oftener than the dollar.

*He is genuinely great who considers himself small and cares nothing about high honors.*
— Thomas À Kempis
1380-1471

*Though your beginning was small, yet your latter end would increase abundantly.*
— Job 8:7

# HOW MUCH OR HOW WELL?

The craftsman requires more time, but his work is more valuable. It is not how much we do, but how well we do it that determines worth. The first measurement of any work is quality. Skill is power, a power which belongs to talent, devotion and patience. It adds stature to life. Monuments are erected to artists— not to bunglers.

Why rush to get out a slipshod job just to pursue more shoddiness in shoddy living? For no one's life is above his work. Haste makes waste, not only of the product, but of the life that turns it out.

*Only those who have the patience to do simple things perfectly will acquire the skill to do difficult things easily.*
— Johann Friedrich von Schiller
1759-1805

*They gave it to the craftsmen and builders to buy hewn stone and timber for beams, and to floor the houses ... And the men did the work faithfully.*
— II Chronicles 34:11,12

*January 10*

# TO IMPROVE THE WORLD

**W**orld improvement is everybody's business. Our mere very presence in the world means we should be a responsible part of it; and that part, good or bad, must of necessity make the world a little better or a little worse.

So— just as you can improve the whole by improving the parts— world improvement must begin with me; and as I succeed in bettering self, I restore the world; for each evil conquered by me is that much of it gone from the world. A few broken habits will make the world more habitable.

*I am to bless the world through what I am.*
— William Makepeace Thackeray
1811 -1863


*For none of us lives to himself,*
*and no man dies to himself.*
— Romans 14:7

*January 11*

# CHANCE OR MISCHANCE

*No* matter which way the ball bounces, it's our game. Play it to win. Yield not to misfortune. We have seen a wrong bounce, a fumbled ball taken for a touchdown on the athletic field— and in the game of life.

Misfortune is real. So is fortune. And on the law of averages there should be enough fortune to more than offset misfortune. But it is not always proportioned that way among all people. The reason— the human factor is more important than the ball's bounce. Fortune comes to those who grab chance and use it, and to those who take mischance and triumph over it. From others it flees.

*We need greater virtues to bear good fortune than bad.*
— Francois de La Rochefoucauld
1613-1680

*We went through fire and through water:*
*but You brought us out to rich fulfillment.*
— Psalm 66:12

# MISTAKES, MESSES AND MISHAPS

All of us make mistakes, but the wise among us are less apt to make them the second time. Though we are human enough to err, one hope for us is our being divine enough to regret it; this means we still have a chance.

In spite of all of mankind's mistakes, messes and mishaps, one thing in our favor is the ability to learn from them. And to learn from blunders is a most practical accomplishment. We make enough errors to get educated, if we acquire knowledge from them. Through this process, fallible people can have a brighter expectation tomorrow. This is reason enough for living!

*Experience enables you to recognize a mistake*
*when you make it again.*
— Franklin P. Jones

*For I have learned by experience.*
— Genesis 30:27

# THE ART OF ADAPTATION

*O*ur world is one of thorns and thistles as well as roses and violets. Practicality demands that we adjust ourselves to both. We can't always have everything just like we want it. Flexibility is required. We must do the best we can. And when thorns prick, we find helpfulness in scenting the perfume with the resolution to be more watchful next time.

Some things about life can be changed to our liking— others can't; and if they can't, then we must change ourselves just to live. This is the art of living— adjustment and readjustment— and it is accomplished by self.

*Better to bend than to break.*
— Scottish Proverb

*I would hasten my escape*
*from the windy storm and tempest.*
— Psalm 55:8

*January 14*

# MADE FOR HELP

"Help! Help me!" These are the words we hear from every nook and corner of the earth. For humanity is in trouble; we hurt; we have needs.

If we can relieve a need, we will always be in demand. Humanity's beaten paths invariably lead to the doors of the helpful.

Whatever your gift—be it soothe the hurting, listening to the fearful, encourage the lonely—give of yourself.

Accordingly, let us render kindness for the same reason a flower blooms—we were made for that purpose.

*Before the judgement seat my service will not be judged by how much I have done, but by how much of me there is in it. No one gives at all until he has given all.*

— A.W. Tozer
1897-1963

*They helped every one his neighbor;
and every one said to his brother,
Be of good courage.*
— Isaiah 41:6

*January 15*

# THE HEARING EAR
# AND SEEING EYE

*E*ars that hear and eyes that see. Great assets. And somewhat uncommon. With them, one can see and observe, hear and perceive. We can get the message of heaven and earth. "The heavens declare the glory of God."

The "tongues in trees" whisper to us that they are known by their fruits. The "books in running brooks" teach us that nature seeks its own level. The "sermons in stones" point up the need of hewing.

We can see good in every thing: even in adversity, which encourages humility, self-examination, adjustment, initiative. We are not fooled by hardship's disguise.

*Sweet are the uses of adversity;*
*Which, like the toad, ugly and venomous,*
*Wears yet a precious jewel in his head;*
*And this our life, exempt from public haunt,*
*Finds tongues in trees, books in the running brooks,*
*Sermons in stones, and good in everything.*

— William Shakespeare
1564-1616

*The hearing ear, and the seeing eye,*
*the Lord has made both of them.*

— Proverbs 20:12

*January 16*

# THE LOCAL JURY

Conscience is the jury in each person's soul which sits in judgment of his conduct. Each case should be tried by the laws of God before we consider our own moral consciousness. But when human behavior is tried in the court of divine laws and pronounced "not guilty" by the jury of conscience, it is then— and only then— that man is free.

No matter what a state or Federal tribunal may say, it's the local jury— deep down in the soul— that really frees or imprisons each person.

O conscience, let me be free and today shall be mine.

*Conscience is thoroughly well-bred and soon leaves off talking to those who do not wish to hear it.*

— Samuel Butler
1612-1680

*...their conscience also bearing witness,*
*and between themselves their thoughts*
*accusing or else excusing them.*

— Romans 2:15

# PRACTICE WHAT YOU PREACH

One Sunday the brother of the minister, a physician, visited the church services. At the conclusion, a lady said to him, "Sir, do you preach, too?"

"No, my brother preaches; I practice," was the reply.

Whether we profess faith in religion, medicine or anything else, a living demonstration of our advocacy will speak louder than anything we say.

It is not amiss, therefore, for us to say, "Preacher, live your sermon; physician, take your medicine." Then we shall listen!

*Practice is the best of all instructors.*
— Publius Syrus
1st Century B. C.

*And how I kept back nothing that was helpful,*
*but proclaimed it to you, and taught you.*
— Acts 20:20

# THE RIGHT THING

Doing right is the measure of civilization's progress. Every step of progress has been by doing right; and every retrogression has been by doing wrong. Right is the solution to the problem; wrong is the problem.

Switching their appearances changes nothing. Reclothing wrong only fashions it in new apparel. Sweeping it under the rug only hides it in deception.

Doing right has its own rewards—not only from God, but from family and friends. I have a friend who is known as a person "who always does the right thing." All of us can be like that if we want.

*God takes notice of clean hands, not full hands.*
— Latin Proverb

*And you shall do what is right*
*and good in the sight of the Lord;*
*that it may be well with you.*
— Deuteronomy 6:18

*January 19*

# LOVE WINS

*L*ove is the winning quality. It wins when everything else fails. We can't win many people by knocking them, nor by fussing with them, nor by embarrassing them, nor by exploiting them, nor by threatening them, nor by freezing them; but we can thaw them and draw them by simply loving them.

Love wins when politics, reason and fear fail. The discerning do not want political treatment. Reason often meets a complete rejection. Fear is apt to answer blow for blow. But love finds hearts receptive; for they see no reason to be wary, feel no need to argue and sense no cause to be afraid.

*Love is the sun against whose melting beams the winter cannot stand. There is not one human being in a million whose clay heart is hardened against love.*

— Henry Allen Tupper

*We love him, because he first loved us.*

— I John 4:19

# RULE YOURSELF

By ruling ourselves we can be kings. More than a king! For he who governs his own life, controls his passions and fears; he reigns in a dominion where kings have often failed.

Losing self-control will enslave a person. It will add to his nervous troubles, multiply his strife, mar his reputation, drive off his friends, erase the smile from his children's faces and take from him his self-respect. We know we don't want that to happen, so we must keep a tight rein on ourselves. For we must either be a king in our own kingdom or a slave in another's.

*The most important thing is to learn to rule oneself.*
— Johann Wolfgang von Goethe
1749-1832

*He who is slow to anger is better than the mighty;*
*and he who rules his spirit than he that takes a city.*
— Proverbs 16:32

# THE ONLY AGE WE HAVE

*E*very age is too rewarding to be wasted. The plan of life is just right: childhood, youth, middle age, old age. Everything comes to us just when we are ready to receive it. To have an age precipitated upon us before we are ready or withheld from us after we are would be most disastrous. Each age has its own peak, and as we get older we can see life from a higher vantage.

Many people exaggerate the past and glorify the future before it arrives. We must live now. It's the only age we have.

*Strike when thou wilt, the hour of rest,*
*But let my last days be my best.*
— Robert Browning
1812 -1889

*If they obey and serve Him,*
*they shall spend their days in prosperity,*
*and their years in pleasures.*
— Job 36:11

# ASPIRATIONS BEFORE ACHIEVEMENT

The supreme incentive to lofty achievement is high objectives. The driving power of an aspiration has lifted many a lowly person. And those who rose were worthy of the elevation for they tried. Their purpose and accomplishments reflect their merit, especially when viewed in the light of noble motives.

Each has the wings to rise, but not every one has the mind to lift himself. We can soar only on aspiring wings that beat, and when they do, our sky knows no limits. What is needed is an aspiration that is not content to be grounded— nor to fly too low.

*Lord, let me not be content*
*With life in trifling service spent*
*Make me aspire!*

— Anonymous

*Do you not know that those who run in a race*
*all run, but one receives the prize?*
*Run in such a way that you may obtain it.*

— I Corinthians 9:24

*January 23*

# THE UNIVERSAL LANGUAGE

If a courteous word or two will make another person feel good, then only a hard-hearted fool will fail to give it to him.

Courtesy is thoughtfulness gently moving from an unselfish heart.

Courtesy will make you liked. It casts a spell as it manifests little acts of attention and consideration, giving others the preference while eating, sitting, standing, walking, in the shop, in the office and at play.

Courtesy is the passport to the world. It is the universal language. Speak it and the world listens. It makes us welcome. Like oil to machinery, it keeps associations running smoothly.

And it doesn't cost anything!

*Nothing is ever lost by courtesy.*
*It is the cheapest of the pleasures; costs nothing*
*and conveys much. It pleases him who gives*
*and him who receives, and thus,*
*like mercy, it is twice blessed.*

— Erastus Wiman

*Love as brothers, be tenderhearted, be courteous.*

— I Peter 3:8

# AND BE CONTENT

*A*void discontent and fret. There is a time to weep and a time to rejoice, but there is no time for a place between the two called discontent.

To the malcontent no house is comfortable, no clothes satisfactory, no job rewarding, no day happy.

The discontented person should ask: "With whom would I swap places, a complete swap, all or none?"

Why waste our energy, time and health to no avail? Contentment will conserve our strength and turn our minds loose to think constructively. But discontent— what a waste!

Peace comes from enjoying what we have and by losing the desire for what we cannot have.

*He is a wise man who does not grieve for the things which he has not, but rejoices for those which he has.*

— Epictetus
55-135

*And be content with such things as you have.*

— Hebrews 13:5

# THE LINKS OF LOYALTY

*O*ne element of character that compensates for a whole lot of weakness is loyalty. Husband and wife demand it, and without it marriage fails. Business success requires it, and devoid of it bankruptcy approaches. National survival necessitates it, and without it doom draws near.

Loyalty is an iron chain of many strong links: love, bravery, self-sacrifice, honesty, truthfulness, steadfastness.

Loyalty is convinced that anything worth obtaining— husband, wife, friend, or any association— is worth retaining and thus is unwavering in its fidelity to the same. Loyalty protects, for it is unafraid. Loyalty perseveres, for it has determination. It's the unfailing spirit that stands the test. It's no traitor!

*His words are bonds;*
*his oaths are oracles;*
*his heart is as far from fraud*
*as heaven from earth.*
— William Shakespeare
1564-1616

*... but showing all good fidelity.*
— Titus 2:10

## MORE THAN A POLICY

"*H*onesty is the best policy," so declared Miguel de Cervantes who lived in the sixteenth century. But honesty is more than policy, more than prudence, more than procedure based primarily on material interest.

While honesty will deal us a better hand in all the affairs of life, it is not played just for gain. It is a principle that is adhered to for honesty's sake because it is right. Doing the honest thing is something the honest person does because he is honest; to be dishonest would be out of character. He's honest, win or lose!

*I am not bound to win, but*
*I am bound to be true.*
*I am not bound to succeed, but*
*I am bound to live up to what light I have.*
— Abraham Lincoln
1809-1865

*You shall not have in your bag differing weights,*
*a heavy and a light. You shall not have in your house*
*differing measures, a large and a small.*
— Deuteronomy 25:13,14

# A LITTLE LOWER THAN ANGELS

*M*an! What a unique creature! A little lower than the angels! So constituted that his possibilities are unlimited!

He is a whole library in one volume.

He is a complete garden hidden in one seed.

With more power than a king, he has dominion over the earth. He can call the plays, provided he stays within the rules of the game. He is the maker of his own destiny, lives where he chooses and how he chooses.

He is the only creature which rises by bowing, for he finds elevation in his subjection to his Maker.

*What a piece of work is a man! how noble in reason!*
*how infinite in faculty! in form and moving*
*how express and admirable! in action how like an angel! in*
*apprehension how like a god!*

— William Shakespeare
1564-1616

*What is man, that You are mindful of him? ...*
*For You have made him a little lower than the angels,*
*and You have crowned him with glory and honor.*

— Psalm 8:4,5

## DEVELOPED BEAUTY

It is better to develop good looks than to be born with them. The most adorable beauty does not wrinkle with the years, or wither at the touch of fever like a drought-stricken flower, or lose its covering like a frost-bitten tree. It is seen more clearly with examination. It is viewed more admiringly with time.

But Socrates called born beauty a short-lived tyranny; Theophrastus, a silent cheat; Theocritus, a delightful prejudice; Plato, a privilege of nature; Homer, a glorious gift of nature; and Ovid, a favor bestowed by the gods.

We can add one thing sure— outward beauty deserves no praise unless matched with the inward charm of self-development.

*Beauty, unaccompanied by virtue,*
*is as a flower without perfume.*
— French Proverb

*As a ring of gold in a swine's snout, so*
*is a lovely woman who lacks discretion.*
— Proverbs 11:22

*January 29*

# THE FRUIT OF SILENCE

*E*veryone needs to steal away for a little while each day to the loneliness of meditation. It gets us off the treadmill of superficial living. It shuts out the noise from the grind of the world and lets us hear the voice that speaks out of silence.

No great work has ever been accomplished without pondering. The world's greats have always sought solitude for musing.

It has been said that Leonardo de Vinci, the renowned artist, would sit almost motionless for days at a time meditating and getting the inspiration for his masterpieces. In musing he nursed his thoughts and was rewarded with greatness.

*The mightiest works of God*
*are the fruit of silence.*
— F.B. Meyer

*Let the words of my mouth,*
*and the meditation of my heart,*
*be acceptable in thy sight,*
*O Lord, my strength, and my redeemer.*
— Psalm 19:14

*January 30*

# LET IT READ ME

*S*hould I read the Bible? Yes! But more importantly I should let it read me. Its philosophies are profoundest. Its counsels are wisest. Its inspirations are loftiest. Its consolations are sweetest. Its goals are highest. Its rebukes are sharpest.

Unopened, the Bible will never read me— nor feed me; but when studied, it will do both. It will glorify the mind, guard the heart, lift the eye, strengthen the hand and guide the feet.

Yes! I should read it to be smart and follow it to be smarter. For of all the Bible versions, the best translation is the one put into action.

*From the time that at my mother's feet
or my father's knee, I learned to lisp verses
from the sacred writings, they have been
my daily study and vigilant contemplation.*
— Daniel Webster
1782-1852

*The entrance of Your words gives light.*
— Psalm 119:130

*January 31*

# AS GOES SELF-RELIANCE

Those who have lost self-reliance have lost all. Without it there is no inspiration; devoid of it there is no courage; free of it there is no concerted effort.

Doubt whom you will, but not God or yourself. They are the two upon whom you must rely the most. Hardly one person in a hundred knows what he can do for himself— with God's help. If the worst should come to worst— if all other assistance should fail— you and He can still make a go of it.

As goes your self-dependence, so goes yourself— up or down.

*To character and success, two things,*
*contradictory as they may seem, must go together—*
*humble dependence and manly independence:*
*humble dependence on God and manly reliance on self.*
— William Wordsworth
1770-1850

*The God of heaven, he will prosper us;*
*therefore we his servants will arise and build.*
— Nehemiah 2:20

*February 1*

## IT'S UP TO US

*H*aving the best in life depends upon me:

- The best thought: we're the offspring of God
- The best book: our Bible read
- The best sermon: the one our good life preaches
- The best quality: love we give and love we receive
- The best play: work we enjoy
- The best cheerfulness: sunshine we scatter
- The best peace: inside each
- The best teacher: our mistakes
- The best way out: the opening we make
- The best gratification: the knowledge
  we have done our work well
- The best day: the one we make

*There's only one corner of the universe
you can be certain of improving and that's your own self.*

Aldous Huxley
1894-1963

*Is not my help in me?*
— Job 6:13

# THE PESSIMIST IT

The pessimist is a loser every way we figure it. He is not mentally prepared to cash in on good things. To him every hill is a mountain, every river is uncrossable, and every star is ready to fall. He walks in shadows when the sun is shining; he hears thunder when there isn't a cloud in sight; and he sips lightly from his glass, thinking the well is going to run dry.

A merchant of gloom, that describes him, but his customers are few. Frankly, I prefer to put my money on the optimist.

*He growled at morning, noon, and night,*
*And trouble sought to borrow;*
*Although today the sky was bright,*
*He knew 'twould storm tomorrow;*
*A thought of joy he could not stand,*
*And struggled to resist it;*
*Though sunshine dappled all the land*
*This sorry pessimist it.*
— Nixon Waterman

*For as he thinketh in his*
*heart, so is he.*
— Proverbs 23:7

*February 3*

# I HAVE DONE WHAT I COULD

In a roaring and flashing thunderstorm, a family gathered into what they thought was the safest room. They huddled in fear. One of them was a little girl who folded her hands, closed her eyes and prayed. Then she confidently said, "Well, I have done what I could."

Oh! how it would add to life if we could say, I have done what I could.

The satisfaction would be most gratifying. Many a person, after living up to some strenuous duty, has been heard to say, "Thank God! I have done my part."

That is the way to climb. The ladder is duty.

*Our grand business is, not to see what lies dimly at a distance, but to do what lies closely at hand.*
— Thomas Carlyle
1795-1881

*She has done what she could.*
— Mark 14:8

# OVERCAUTION DOES NOTHING

*S*uccess climbs its ladder cautiously, but overcaution never gets off the ground. The one who is so wary that he is afraid to try for fear he will fail has already failed.

Overcaution is too much of a good thing, just like no caution is too much of a bad thing. Stop all risks and you stop the world: the sailing of ships, the drilling for oil, the sowing of seeds and the harvesting of crops.

The good life has its hazards; and blessed is he who lives it carefully— but lives it!

*Who waits until the wind shall silent keep*
*Will never find the ready hour to sow;*
*Who watcheth clouds will have no time to reap.*
— Helen Hunt Jackson

*He who observes the wind will not sow,*
*and he who regards the clouds will not reap.*
— Ecclesiastes 11:4

# MONEY IS WHAT WE MAKE IT

*O*ne of the strongest influences in this world is the love of money. Shouldn't be, but is. Yet money within itself is not bad. It is rather good, but it's the bad people who cause it to take on the appearance of themselves.

Without doubt, our attitude toward money contributes much to our happiness or sorrow, peace or discontent; for many of our blessings or curses center around it, depending on what we make it— servant or master.

*Money can buy the husk of many things,*
*but not the kernel. It brings you food,*
*but not appetite; medicine, but not health;*
*acquaintances, but not friends; servants,*
*but not faithfulness; days of joy,*
*but not peace and happiness.*
— Henrik Ibsen
1828-1906


*For the love of money is the root*
*of all evil.*
— I Timothy 6:10

*February 6*

# SUCH AGREEABLE FRIENDS

The bristly dog is not much for agreement. That's all right, but it's his disagreeable way of expressing it that repels us. We prefer the agreeable dog; he's not so beastly.

And our choices of people are no different— not that all have to conform to our views, but we do demand that they be agreeable.

The practical thought for me is: The world is filled with would-be friends I haven't won and never will by barking and biting. The behavior that wins them is affable and amiable, conversable and considerate— not frictional.

*Animals are such agreeable friends.*
*They ask no questions; they pass no criticisms.*
— George Eliot
1819 -1880

*Let each one of us please his neighbor*
*for his good, leading to edification.*
— Romans 15:2

*February 7*

# THE STRAITS OF ECONOMY

*O*ur ship won't come in except through the Straits of Economy. We can increase our wealth by decreasing our wants. We can raise our wages by lowering our expenses. We can have more by wasting less. What we make is not as important as how we handle it.

This requires efficiency, planning and the maturity to stick with the plans. Economy does not mean no spending—it means wise spending. Frugality takes the view that a thing not needed is too high at any price. And there are so many things we don't need!

*Economy is in itself a source*
*of great revenue.*
— Lucius Annaeus Seneca
8 B.C.-65 A.D.

*The younger son. . . wasted his possessions. . .*
*and he began to be in want.*
— Luke 15:13,14

*February 8*

# WHAT DO YOU SEE?

As a battle was being fought, a general said to a private, "Soldier, what do you see?"

"A lost battle, sir," was the reply.

The general responded, "Where you see failure, I see triumph."

It is amazing how much difference there is in what people see. Where one views a village, another a city; where one beholds ugliness, another beauty; and where one sees defeat, another victory. The difference is in the people— not the things they behold. The sights are fairer to those with deeper insights. And backbone gives them special lenses.

*Poor eyes limit your sight;*
*poor vision limits your deeds.*
— Franklin Field

*Eyes have they, but they see not.*
— Psalm 115:5

*February 9*

# GENEROSITY

$\mathcal{I}$ can make today mine by being generous. To receive and receive and never give puts a blight on us, for it is a perversion of the flow of blessings. The earth gives to each and we in return must give to others to strike a noble balance, without which the hoarder suffers the greatest loss— the loss of self-respect, usefulness and happiness.

Our attitude toward giving demonstrates our attitude toward life: toward ourselves, our neighbor, and the Great Giver. Toward self the donor is unselfish; toward his neighbor he is sympathetic; and toward God he is grateful.

*Give what you have.*
*To someone it may be better than you dare think.*
— Henry Wadsworth Longfellow
1807-1882

*For I was hungry and you gave Me food;*
*I was thirsty and you gave Me drink;*
*I was a stranger and you took Me in.*
— Matthew 25:35

# LEARNING TO BE ME

*B*e natural! The only way to be somebody is to be ourself. Trying to wear another's personality— look and act like him— is hard at first and becomes impossible later. A comical, obnoxious sham! And what the pretender doesn't know is, his imitation personality is nearly as hard to sell as false faces would be to angels.

In the drama of life we are cast in only one role— ourself— and we should play it, not imitate another. This does not bar improvements, but make them as the real person you are. I need to learn to be me. No one else is as well qualified as I am.

*Be yourself, and be the person you hope to be.*
— Robert Louis Stevenson
1850-1894

*Now therefore present yourselves*
*before the Lord.*
— I Samuel 10:19

*February 11*

# WHEN DONKEYS TRY TO SING

*If* God bestows varied talents on different people—and He does— then it is wise for us to do the thing for which we are best fitted. This is why it is best for the donkey to bray and the bird to sing— each has that gift.

Success comes easier when we do what we were cut out to do. The world never looks empty to the one who finds his place and fills it. Using our capability will make us more capable; but burying our talent will start a cemetery in our own lives.

*If you have a talent, use it in every which way possible.*
*Don't hoard it. Don't dole it out like a miser. Spend it*
*lavishly like a millionaire intent on going broke.*
— Brendan Francis

*. . .to each according to his*
*own ability.*
— Matthew 25:15

*February 12*

# A WISE RULER

Abraham Lincoln's own words bespeak his greatness:

- His love for the common people: "God must be a lover of the common people, or he would not have made so many of them."
- His honesty: "If, in your judgment, you cannot be an honest lawyer, resolve to be honest without being a lawyer."
- His commitment to right: "I am not bound to win, but I am bound to be true. I am not bound to succeed, but I am bound to live up to what light I have."
- His compassion and foresight: "I believe this nation cannot endure permanently half slave and half free."
- His resolution: ". . .that we here highly resolve that these dead shall not have died in vain. . ."
- His trust in God: "Without the assistance of the Divine Being. . . I cannot succeed. With that assistance I cannot fail!"

*And having thus chosen our course, let us renew our trust in God and go forward without fear and with manly hearts.*
— Abraham LIncoln
1809-1865

*Select a discerning and wise man, and set him over the land.*
— Genesis 41:33

*February 13*

# MORE VALUABLE THAN WEALTH

Health is more valuable than wealth; without it, all people are poor. The world turns at such a fast pace an unhealthy body has trouble keeping up. Regrettable but true, the world has blessings the sickly person finds hard to enjoy.

So— after spirituality— put health at the top of your priority list. For money is of little value to the person who has lost health. What's the point in having delicious food you can't eat? A luxury car in which you can't ride? Or a big house when you are confined to one room— a sick room?

*Look to your health; if you have it, praise God,*
*and value it next to a good conscience;*
*for health is the second blessing*
*that we mortals are capable of;*
*a blessing that money cannot buy.*
— Izzak Walton
1593-1683

*Beloved, I pray that you may prosper in all things*
*and be in health, just as your soul prospers.*
— III John 2

*February 14*

# WHAT LOVE FEELS

*L*ove is the digitalis of the heart— the world's most powerful stimulant. It is the stimulus to climb mountains, swim rivers, wade snows, cross deserts, sleep in the cold, work in the heat, and through it all whisper, "You are my Love."

It is the slowest and quickest quality: Slowest to doubt— quickest to believe. Slowest to criticize— quickest to approve. Slowest to irritate— quickest to smile. Slowest to accuse— quickest to excuse.

Love is the whole world, but only for lovers.

*Love is the one treasure that multiplies by division. It is the one gift that grows bigger the more you take from it. It is the one business in which it pays to be an absolute spendthrift. You can give it away, throw it away, empty your pockets, shake the basket, turn the glass upside down, tomorrow you will have more than ever.*

— Anonymous

*And Jacob loved Rachel.*
— Genesis 29:18

# NOT EVEN A CAMEL

*B*urdens are not so burdensome when they are laid aside at night. It's bearing them day and night that kills. Not even a camel can hold up long at that. What we need is not lighter burdens so much as rested backs.

Practical living requires us to put away our burdens at night. The chances are most of them will look lighter in the morning; if not, we will be stronger to face them after a night's rest.

*The camel, at the close of day,*
*Kneels down upon the sandy plain*
*To have his burden lifted off*
*And rest again.*

*My soul, thou too should to thy knees*
*When daylight draweth to a close,*
*And let thy Master lift the load*
*And grant repose.*

— Anonymous

*Cast your burden upon the Lord,*
*and He shall sustain you.*
— Psalm 55:22

# BAD COMPANY

An old parrot flew out of a farm house and joined some crows in a watermelon field. The farmer, not knowing this and wanting to protect the fruit of his labors, blasted them with his shotgun. The results were three dead crows and one ruffled parrot with a missing toe.

The farmer tenderly took him home where the excited children gathered around and asked, "What happened?"

"Bad company! Bad company"! answered the parrot.

He spoke wiser than he knew. His foolish choice of associates had endangered him.

So it is with us— bad days come from bad companions, and better days come from better associates.

*'Tis better to be alone than in bad company.*
— George Washington
1732-1799

*He who walks with wise men will be wise:*
*but the companion of fools will be destroyed.*
— Proverbs 13:20

*February 17*

# FAITHFUL IN SMALL MATTERS

Fidelity in small things is at the base of every great life. The way we handle the small things shows our character for the big things. Such consequences come from little causes, which maybe are not so little after all.

An old sailor expressed it: "A ship may be sunk by a cargo of sand, as well as by a cargo of millstones." In that event, the little grains of sand are not so little. Thus, the things that are thought to be little are big enough to float us or sink us.

*In great matters men show themselves
as they wish to be seen;
in small matters, as they are.*
— Gamaliel Bradford

*He who is faithful in what is least
is faithful also in much;
and he who is unjust in what is least
is unjust also in much.*
— Luke 16:10

# HAVING REQUIRES STRIVING

When I was a small boy on the farm, someone in the family (which often meant me) had to do the churning. More valuable than the butter was the lesson that having requires doing, that very little comes to us except through exertion.

One reason we do not find more valuables is our inadequate search. We quit too soon. Our world has its good things, but ordinarily they are not on the surface nor in shallow water; obtaining them requires thought and work and patience. We can't have the butter without churning the milk, nor the kernel without husking the corn.

*When love and skill work together, expect a masterpiece.*

— John Ruskin

1819-1900

*He said to Simon, "Launch out into the deep,
and let down your nets for a catch."*

— Luke 5:4

# HOW TO HANDLE GOOD FORTUNE

We must develop ourselves on the inside until we are big enough to handle promotions and riches. If we are not big enough for good fortune, we will be better off if it never comes; for it has destructive and diverse effects on little people. It swells their heads and shrinks their hearts. It makes them rich but poor. While they have money to spend, it won't buy what they need.

But recovery is always in sight because good fortune will not go far unless accompanied by sense. Let's never forget— sense can outrun money any day.

*It requires greater virtue
to sustain good fortune than bad.*
— La Rochefoucauld
1613-1680

*There is one who makes himself rich,
yet has nothing;
and one who makes himself poor,
yet has great riches.*
— Proverbs 13:7

*February 20*

# WHY COMPARE YOURSELF?

*C*omparing your life with others is hurtful, useless and foolish. If you match your life with inferiors, it brings a perverted satisfaction which means nothing. And if you liken it to superiors, it creates discontent by focusing attention on what you don't have.

Why compare? You wouldn't swap lives if you could because it involves taking on another's health, disposition, appetite, habits, friends, loves, hates, sorrows, interests— not just his talent or wealth. For us, success and happiness are found in being ourselves and in living our own lives in whatever state we are compelled to live it.

> *Enjoy your life without comparing it*
> *with that of another.*
> — Marquis de Condorcet

> *But they, measuring themselves by themselves,*
> *and comparing themselves among themselves,*
> *are not wise.*
> — II Corinthians 10:12

# LIVING FOR OTHERS

Others! The ones we love! What a motivating power for struggling on! And this is not lower-class, middle-class or upper-class morality. This is the force of love which is true wherever you find this age-old quality.

Loyalty to others will not let us quit. It causes men and women to search their souls for a little extra strength, which they find and which spurs them on to glorious victory in the face of seeming defeat. And this devotion which holds the welfare of others dearer than life will prompt them, if need be, to give the last heart-beat in their defense.

*The princes among us are those who forget themselves and serve mankind.*
— Woodrow Wilson
1856-1924

*I will lay down my life for your sake.*
— John 13:37

# WORTHY TO RULE

When a person treasures the rights of men— as Washington did; and prefers principle to profit— as Washington preferred; and believes "that man was not designed by the All-wise Creator to live for himself alone"— as Washington believed; and is courageous enough to stand up to opposition— as Washington stood; and towers above trickery and partisanship— as Washington towered; and refuses to be a king— as Washington refused; and trusts in "the All-wise Disposer of events"— as Washington trusted; and sees heroics in ragged men with a cause— as Washington saw— that person is truly worthy of rulership and a place "in the hearts of his countrymen."

*The red coats do look best, but it takes*
*the ragged boys to do the fighting.*
— George Washington
1732 -1799

*Moreover you shall select from all the people able men,*
*such as fear God, men of truth, hating covetousness;*
*and place such over them, to be rulers.*
— Exodus 18:21

# A BRAINY AFFAIR

*R*eading is a brainy affair: we use our own and borrow the author's. It is a dual mental exercise whereby we increase our power by using and feeding our brains.

Speaking of power, most of ours is from the eyes up. Accordingly, a great opportunity to increase human force is in reading. The mightiness of good books is given to those who study them.

We cannot live by bread alone or TV or chit-chat or even work. Our nature calls for progress. And a few moments of profound reading each day will give us the necessary information and motivation for growth.

*The man who does not read good books
has no advantage over the man who cannot read at all.*
— Mark Twain
1835-1910

*Give attention to reading. . .*
— I Timothy 4:13

*February 24*

# LEARN AND LIVE

Live and learn, but more importantly, learn and live—that's my motto. Let's take the lessons in the right order: First, know yourself. Second, know what you ought to do. Third, know what is needed to make you do it.

All around us are contributory lessons to these three. There are teaching tongues everywhere: in the literate and illiterate, in the young and old, in friends and enemies. There are enlightening books in everything; in remembrance and forgetfulness, in happiness and sorrow, in harmony and discord, in thrift and waste, in trial and error, in victory and defeat. No question about the teachers. What about the students?

*I grow old learning something new every day.*

— Solon
638 (?)-559 B.C.

*Take firm hold of instruction,*
*do not let go; keep her, for she is your life.*
— Proverbs 4:13

# ERR ONLY IN JUDGMENT

*E*very time the ball carrier takes the ball he runs the risk of fumbling. And in this game called life, we also run the risk of poor judgment every time we use it. But if we don't, we never will reach the goal line.

Mistakes being the common lot of humanity, we are sure to make some; however, we have humanity's sympathy, provided our hearts are true. At times our judgment is sure to prove itself blind; but if that is the only mistake— judgment— and the world sees in us no baseness, it is apt to be rather tolerant. For the motive puts every error in a new perspective.

*We are eager for the right;*
*O ye who lead; take heed!*
*Blindness we may forgive,*
*But baseness we will smite.*

— William Vaughn Moody

*But I obtained mercy,*
*because I did it ignorantly.*

— I Timothy 1:13

# IN THE STRUGGLE

*W*e never fail if we really try to succeed. Though we do not reach the set goal, we reach several rewards just for the trying.

Not all who dig for gold find it, but they do strengthen their character and their resolve and their muscles. The struggle is more valuable than the prize. Truly, man owes his well-being to that striving the world calls effort. While the struggle grips his attention and absorbs his interest, it adds to his enthusiasm, drive and contentment.

Consequently, if I maintain the forward pace, keeping my eye on the goal— come what may— I am sure to be a winner.

*Everything requires effort: the only thing you can achieve without it is failure.*
— Anonymous

*Let your eyes look straight ahead,*
*and your eyelids look right before you.*
— Proverbs 4:25

# *February 27*

## QUIT? NEVER!

*T*here is indescribable gratification in being able to say: "I have done it— this thing I sought to do— I have done it." It is a tribute to constancy that stickability carries us through our adversities and lifts us over our obstacles, even those which appear insurmountable.

Consistency finally wins. If you are knocked down, don't give up— get up; and if you can't get up, crawl. It is all right to stop long enough to get your breath, but don't surrender. The victory goes not to the person who is the least hit, but to the one who won't quit.

*Press on! Nothing in the world can take the place*
*of perseverance. Talent will not; nothing is more common*
*than unsuccessful men with talent. Genius will not;*
*unrewarded genius is almost a proverb. Education will not;*
*the world is full of educated derelicts.*
— Calvin Coolidge
1872 -1933

*And let us not grow weary while doing good,*
*for in due season we shall reap if we do not lose heart.*
— Galatians 6:9

*February 28*

# THE POWER TO FORGET

*F*orget it! Ah! what power to rid our hearts of anxiety and anguish.

Some cruel deed has wounded you, forget it; don't think of it again.

An unprecipitated harsh or unjust sentence has irritated you, let it rest; the guilty one may have only given vent to some pent up nervousness, and will be pleased to see it forgotten.

Some unproved scandal is about to estrange you from an old friend, forget it and thus prove your charity and preserve your peace of mind.

A suspicious look threatens to cool your affection, forget it; better still, return it with a look of trust that restores confidence.

*A retentive memory is a good thing, but the ability to forget is the true token of greatness.*
— Elbert Hubbard
1856-1915

*For You have cast all my sins behind Your back.*
— Isaiah 38:17

*March 1*

# THE SCHOOL OF LIFE

When we view life as a school, we can better pass the tests to which we are subjected, knowing that as we excel in each crisis we demonstrate more fitness to advance to a higher grade.

In some tests we don't make "A"; once in a while we fail; but as long as we are in school— a lifetime— we still have an opportunity for improvement. Some of the lessons are hard to learn; but with the penalty for failing so bitter and the reward for passing so big, we usually wise up somewhat before school closes.

*Lord, let me make this rule:*
*To think of life as school,*
*And try my best*
*To stand each test,*
*And do my work*
*And nothing shirk.*
— Maltbie D. Babcock

*Or speak to the earth*
*and it will teach you.*
— Job 12:8

# SUCCESS FORMULIZED

*F*ormula for success:

- Know yourself
- Take time to think
- Use good judgment
- Make plans
- Be optimistic— talk like a winner
- Give yourself to your task
- Learn to say no
- Amend your faults
- Get up when knocked down
- Love God and man

*Success comes to those who are neither afraid to fail nor discouraged by failures.*

— Anonymous

*A desire accomplished is sweet to the soul.*

— Proverbs 13:19

# BETTER THAN CHANCE

*I*f chance gives you an even break, that is fair enough. Man loves chance, but chance seldom loves him. Luck sometimes grants favors, but planned concerted effort grants more.

There are many things chance won't do: won't grow a crop, won't build a house, won't operate a business, won't write a book, won't earn a college degree, won't save a dollar. Doing worthwhile things have to be done on purpose.

The winner is not willing for luck to deal his portion. As the captain of his fate, he rides the waves of fortune determined to make some luck for himself— and he does!

> *Those who trust to chance must abide*
> *by the results of chance.*
> — Calvin Coolidge

> *And Solomon determined to build a house. . .*
> — II Chronicles 2:1

# JOURNEY OF DECISIONS

Life is a journey of decisions and the person who can't make them has a hard trip ahead. All along the pathway of life are stalled persons, stuck between yes and no.

When Alexander was asked how he conquered the world, he replied, "By not delaying."

One must have a mind before he can make it up, but indecision usually stems not from a lack of intelligence but from a lack of faith and courage and diligence. For the better life, be wise enough, confident enough, bold enough and industrious enough, to make decisions, and then be resolute enough to carry them out.

*Who hesitate and falter life away,*
*And lose tomorrow the ground won today.*
— Matthew Arnold
1822-1888

*How long will you falter between two opinions?*
— I Kings 18:21

*March 5*

# ASPIRE

Of the qualities that distinguish the big, the little and the mediocre, one is their aspiration. Massive accomplishments cannot come from tiny aims.

The climber must upward turn his face. Ambition invites our steps and points us to higher places.

Goals add life to life. With no goals, man dies of nothing.

If tongues could be put in all the failures of men and women, they would say: "You didn't aspire. You didn't climb. You didn't continue."

So, for a blaze of success, we each should pick our star, hitch to it, and then hold on.

*Vision looks inward and becomes a duty.*
*Vision looks outward and becomes aspiration.*

— Stephen Wise
1874-1949

*I must also see Rome.*

— Acts 19:21

# LIKE A CACTUS BLOSSOM

Though victory is sweet, it can come only from conflict. And the rainbow which is beautiful is formed solely in a cloud.

So it is with us: The triumphant and comely emerge stronger and prettier from the conflicts and storms. They succumb not to the hideous influences which threaten them. They can prevail and they do. They can be better men and women and that they become. Like the cactus blossom, a marvel of sweetness, they rise above a prickly mass of ugliness. They become winners by exerting the greater dominance.

*He that wrestles with us strengthens our nerves
and sharpens our skill. Our antagonist is our helper.*
— Edmund Burke
1729-1797

*Be not overcome of evil,
but overcome evil with good.*
— Romans 12:21

*March 7*

# THE WRONG VIEW OF LIFE

A sailor boy slides over the side of his ship, a deserter. Why? He thought all a sailor had to do was to board his ship and sail, sail, sail, until finally he lands in a foreign port and there beneath a full moon, amidst glamour and luxury, court a native beauty in a romantic land. Instead, he ended up scrubbing decks and washing dishes. A false ideal ruined him.

And his error is society's error— a perverted notion of the ends of living. The doctrine of effortless ease— eat, drink and be merry— has left us unprepared to face the sterner requirements of life.

*There has never yet been a man in our*
*history who led a life of ease whose*
*name is worth remembering.*
— Theodore Roosevelt

*Man shall not live by bread alone. . .*
— Matthew 4:4

# LIKE GRASSHOPPERS

A city man visited his cousin in the country. Together they walked over the crops. After they had inspected the corn, the city cousin enthusiastically commented, "Never have I seen corn like this. Surely this must be the finest corn in the state."

The farmer pessimistically muttered, "Yes, but it is so hard on the soil." Good had sprung out of the ground, but to him it was only a sign of hidden disaster. His own outlook had denied him the happiness his success deserved.

Nothing is too good to be true, if we expect good; but there is no hope up ahead, if we expect failure.

*To expect defeat is nine-tenths of defeat itself.*
— Francis Marion Crawford

*And we were like grasshoppers in our own sight,*
*and so we were in their sight.*
— Numbers 13:33

*March 9*

## BEARING BURDENS

Actual burdens only keep our feet on the ground, but it is the over-burden complex that bends our heads to the ground where it is difficult to see life's possibilities. It is hard to see a star when our heads are down.

We can find courage to raise up— and, surprisingly, the burdens won't be as heavy as we think— realizing that the other fellow lives with his problems which are just as numerous and complex as ours. And if he can, we can. This will save us from self-pity which will break anybody.

*If all the world's secret troubles were put in one pile*
*and each person asked to take an equal share,*
*we would surely prefer to keep those we already have.*

— Socrates
469-399 B.C.

*We are hard pressed on every side, yet not crushed;*
*we are perplexed, but not in despair.*
— II Corinthians 4:8

## SORROW IS IN THE PLAN

*S*orrow is a part of the world's plan; sooner or later it visits all. But not all of us react in the same way. Some mellow; others harden. It can beautify your life like the dew gives the flower a more beautiful hue. Grief can cause us to be more compassionate, increase our sincerity and bring us closer to reality.

Sadness must be for the good of humanity, or we would not have been given the capacity for it, but so is joy. Sorrow is so potent, however, that we need it only in small amounts for brief periods, but we require joy in big doses for long durations.

*God sometimes washes the eyes of his children*
*with tears in order that they may read aright*
*his providence and his commandments.*
— Theodore Cuyles
1822-1909

*. . .as the month which was turned*
*from sorrow to joy for them,*
*and from mourning to a holiday.*
— Esther 9:22

# PAIN PROTECTS

Pain has been ordained for the protection and enhancement of us all. Without it, we wouldn't know whether we were walking on green grass or hot coals, on sharp nails or feather pillows.

Seeing that hurts of many kinds, from many sources, are appointed to every one of us as God has thought wise, then my part is to thicken my skin for lashes, adjust my mind for injury, strengthen my back for burdens, and increase my faith for sorrow.

And each time I suffer by trial, I shall be a lot more human and a little more divine— and prepared for a little more pain.

*There's a pang in all rejoicing,*
*and a joy in the heart of pain.*
— Bayard Taylor
1825-1878

*For we know that the whole creation groans*
*and labors with birth pangs together until now.*
— Romans 8:22

## SPEAKING AND LISTENING

*S*ilence is not always better than speech, but it is always good enough for us to think twice before we break it.

The better thing is to be discerning enough to know when to talk and when to listen. Nothing marks a person quicker than his tongue and ears, what he says and what he doesn't say.

A good rule to follow is: If our words are not worth more than our silence, don't waste them. And in the event we should violate the first rule, then follow the second: If we talk ourselves into trouble, we should listen ourselves out of it.

*There are two sciences*
*which every man ought to learn:*
*First, the silence of speech;*
*second, the more difficult one of silence.*

— Socrates
469-399 B.C.

*. . .a time to keep silence and*
*a time to speak.*
— Ecclesiastes 3:7

## LOVE UNDERSTANDS

The little world each lives in needs an atmosphere of understanding. This calls for artists— not bunglers. To understand people is truly one of the most accomplished arts and one of the most necessary ingredients of successful living.

It is an art more dependent on heart feeling than eye sight and ear hearing. We cannot fathom people unless we have the love that feels for them and with them. It is then that we place the charitable construction on their motives, magnify their virtues and minimize their faults. When this is done, there is no problem in understanding people.

*Love is the one ingredient of which our world never tires*
*and which there is never an abundance.*
*It is needed in the marketplace and in the mansions.*
*It is needed in the ghettos and in the governments.*
*It is needed in homes, in hospitals and individual hearts.*
*The world will never out grow its need for love.*

— C. Neil Strait

*For love shall cover a multitude of sins.*

— I Peter 4:8

# POWER STEERING

There is something lacking in the person who can control his dog better than himself. It makes us wonder which one is living the dog's life.

Evidently it takes more power to steer ourselves than other people or beasts. In giving an order to self, you know if you really mean it or not .

Those who rule themselves are the most masterly masters. Being free, they are unshackled to handle today and unchained to face tomorrow. They direct themselves, and that's where success or failure begins.

The world is yours, provided you are yours.

*Self-control is the ability to keep cool
while someone is making it hot for you.*
— Anonymous

*And everyone who competes for the prize
is temperate in all things*
— I Corinthians 9:25

## RIGHT— THE SAFE WAY

*T*he right of way in living belongs to those who pursue right. No person should expect to run the barricade of wrong for long without crashing. History testifies that safety is on the side of those who follow the traffic rules of moral correctness.

But not all will choose the correct way. Of course, every person has a right to his rights— though they are wrongs— unless they hurt others. But his having this privilege settles nothing, other than his claim to personal freedom. For no question is ever answered until it is answered right.

*Heaven itself has ordained the right.*
— George Washington
1732-1799

*I will teach you the good*
*and the right way.*
— I Samuel 12:23

# CONSCIENCE-MADE PRISONS

*H*ow unfortunate for a person to make a prison for himself out of his own conscience— a prison stronger than iron bars. For no dungeon can be as frightening and unyielding as one's locked up conscience. No jailer can be as unrelenting as one's self. No chains can be as restrictive as a mind shackled with self-condemnation.

Though we live in the land of the free, we are not liberated unless our conscience is free and clear. The freest freedom is within us. And accordingly each who would have it must keep himself fit to live with.

*Labor hard to keep alive in your breast*
*that little spark of celestial fire*
*called conscience.*
— George Washington
1732-1799

*I myself always strive to have a conscience*
*without offense toward God and men.*
— Acts 24:16

# WHAT A COMBINATION

*S*landerous tongues! Slanderous ears! The combination which gives slander to the wind. It spreads where sweet misery seeks companionship. Where unclean people seek to be cleaner. Where the defeated and frustrated wish to knock others down for their stairs.

Having no joy in goodness, this destroyer of reputations finds delight in another's destruction. With death as his trade, he would make a good hangman, if it were not for his cowardice. But this would expose him.

To noble souls, the slanderer's malignment is a dagger to their ears and a sword to their hearts. And they flee him, leaving him no friends but his own kind.

*A lot of molehills become mountains*
*when someone adds a little dirt.*
— Ancient Proverb

*Whoever secretly slanders his neighbor,*
*him will I cut off.*
— Psalm 101: 5

# NOT EVERYONE HAS A PRICE

*N*o! Not every person has his price. Some cannot be bought. Those who can, put the price tag on themselves— not on employer, not on a friend, not on a confidant— for in selling another, they sell themselves.

When we start grading lost power in human relations, we have to put disloyalty up toward the top of the list. For when trust breaks down, our whole world quits turning.

If we are going to be another's friend, for heaven's sake we should never betray them. Be true. Give others the quiet confidence in you they need.

> *Still, as of old,*
> *Man by himself is priced.*
> *For thirty pieces Judas sold*
> *Himself, not Christ.*
> — Anonymous

> *And they counted out to him*
> *thirty pieces of silver. And from that time*
> *he sought opportunity to betray Him.*
> — Matthew 26:15, 16

*March 19*

# THE OPPORTUNITIES OF AGE

*A*ge presents opportunities that youth, because of inexperience, is not prepared to accept. Experience comes only with time. We would not sell intellectualism and zeal short. Neither would we undervalue experience; for it has tested numerous theories, many of which proved to be jokers for youth.

There is no substitute for gray matter, nor for gray hair. Combine the two and you have double power; add to them zeal and you have a triple threat. Youth can have the two, but not the three. Age can have them all.

> *An age so blest that, by its side,*
> *Youth seems the waste instead.*
>
> — Robert Browning
> 1812 -1889

> *But he rejected the counsel which the elders*
> *gave him, and consulted the young men*
> *who had grown up with him.*
>
> — I Kings 12:8

# A NATURAL RELAXER

*T*ake care that the face which looks out from your mirror in the morning is a pleasant one. You may not see it again all day, but others will— and it will attract or repel.

We may have more brains than our competitor; but if he smiles and we frown, he will find open doors where we find them closed.

A smile is a natural relaxer for the one who does it and for the one who sees it. A friend-maker. A source of health, comfort and happiness for everybody.

*If you meet a person with no smile,*
*why not give him yours.*
— Anonymous

*Saul and Jonathan were beloved*
*and pleasant in their lives.*
— II Samuel 1:23

# BEAUTIFUL WORLD

There is so much beauty in the world: Majestic mountains. Sleeping valleys. Rolling plains. Winding rivers. Billowy oceans. Blue skies. Silvery moon. Twinkling stars. Green grass. Colorful flowers. Picturesque trees. Good looking animals. Graceful fowls.

The only ugliness we have in this world is humanity's conduct, humanity's litter and humanity's abuse of the beautiful. But the world does have its adorable people who live becoming lives. They are the world's masterpieces of unequalled beauty, an adorableness we make of ourselves; and the more we develop, the more we behold. For much of the beauty mankind sees is only a mirror reflecting self.

*A thing of beauty is a joy forever.*
— John Keats
1795 -1821

*He has made everything*
*beautiful in His time.*
— Ecclesiastes 3:11

# ARE WE REFLECTING SELF?

"What a frightful neighborhood," said Grandma Alarmist.

"A sorry people," commented Grandpa Faultfinder.

"So overbearing," harangued Aunt Browbeater.

"They're criminals," stated Cousin Skeleton- N- Closet.

Then Uncle Number-One remarked, "Never before saw such a selfish group."

"A dreadful bore, these dull people," protested Son Stupid.

"It's a concentration of stuck-ups," stated older Daughter Frosty.

"They're no good," spouted the parrot.

But Mrs. Sunshine had the opposite view: "Good people, considerate, kind, unselfish, and they are smart."

Oftentimes what we see is only a mirror reflecting self. The world looks better when seen through better eyes.

*If we had no faults of our own,*
*we would not take so much pleasure*
*in noticing those of others.*
— La Rochefoucauld
1613 -1680

*You are the man.*
— II Samuel 12:7

## A LITTLE SUGAR INSIDE

*A*s a loving mother pressed her little boy to her bosom, she asked, "Johnny, what makes you so sweet and cheerful?"

Johnny replied, "I think when God made me out of dust, he must have put a little sugar in."

Johnny isn't a philosopher— or is he?— just a first-grader. Nevertheless, he expressed the secret of a sweet disposition— sugar on the inside. The pleasant, cheerful temperament is only the outward manifestation of an inward state. Both the best and the worst, the sweetest and the bitterest, are in the mind. Sweeten it to your advantage, for the power of a good-humored personality is inconceivable.

*What sweet delight a quiet life affords.*
— William Drummond
1585-1649

*David. . . the sweet psalmist of Israel.*
— II Samuel 23:1

# ABHOR AND CLING

*O*ne sure lesson history teaches is: The more association with evil, the less evil it appears. The commonness of vice makes it seem harmless and respectable. But neither ugliness gets pretty nor wrong right, we just get accustomed to viewing them. We are the ones who change, not the evils we once decried. Thus through a gradual process, our environment can tempt the purest to pursue the things they once despised.

Lest we come to adore what we now abhor, may we refrain from taking the simple but deadly steps: association with evil, condonation of evil, approval of evil, embrace of evil and addiction to evil.

*Evil can never be undone, but only purged and redeemed.*
— Dorothy L. Sayers

*Abhor what is evil.*
*Cling to what is good.*
— Romans 12:9

## NO GLORY SEEKING

*T*he glory-seeker is some actor, but a poor box office attraction. In his theatrics he sings his own praises, which are an annoying solo. He is nothing but a strutting performer whose conceit bores his audience. He wishes to blossom, but deflowers himself. Desiring to be a giant, he makes himself a dwarf. While none of us can wear his hat, just any of us can fill his shoes.

What a wonderful person this would-be wishes us to see, and this we could see, if he would be only an as-is. For there is eminence in being our honored self, our humble, sincere, unselfish self.

*Things average out: if you think too much*
*of yourself, other people will not.*
— Anonymous

*A man's pride will bring him low;*
*but the humble in spirit will retain honor.*
— Proverbs 29:23

# THE TENDERHEARTED

ompassion is a deep-hearted, big-hearted quality. It is the ability to feel with others in their needs. It identifies with the pain of another's misery, the wound of their sorrow, the anguish of their concern, or the wants of their poverty.

It is one thing the whole human family needs and craves— mercy. And those who fill that need will find doors that swing inward to their approach.

*Pity weeps and runs away:*
*Compassion comes to help and stay.*
— Janet Curtis O'Leary

*Finally, all of you be of one mind,*
*having compassion for one another;*
*love as brothers, be tenderhearted, be courteous.*
— I Peter 3:8

*March 27*

# WHAT DO I THINK OF ME?

*W*hat do I think of me? Believe it or not, it means more than what the world thinks. The approval I need most is from the person I see in the mirror. That is the person I work with, play with, eat with, sleep with and shall die with— what he or she thinks of me is most important. If that person doesn't approve, then the recognition and approbation of all others mean nothing.

The greatest characters have always prized self-esteem above public opinion. Being able to look ourselves in the eye is better than the fickle notice of onlookers.

*What I am, what I am not, in the eye of the world,*
*is what I never cared for much.*
— Robert Browning
1812-1889

*. . .not with eyeservice, as men pleasers,*
*but in sincerity of heart, fearing God.*
— Colossians 3:22

# PUT-OFF DAYS

*P*rocrastination is the art of putting off what we should get on. It has no future, and come to think of it— no present nor past.

Today is the golden opportunity, tomorrow the silvery chance, and the next day the brazen improbability, and the day beyond that the iron impossibility.

All such put-off days quickly turn into yesterdays while immobile men and women stand on feet of clay that soon turn to dust.

*Putting off an easy thing makes it hard.*
*Putting off a hard thing makes it impossible*
— George Larimer

*Do you not say, "There are still four months*
*and then comes the harvest"?*
*. . .lift up your eyes and look at the fields,*
*for they are already white for harvest!*
— John 4:35

*March 29*

# MARKINGS OF CHARACTER

$\mathcal{D}$iogenes the Cynic (400-325 B.C.) is reputed to have walked the streets, carrying a lantern, as if he were searching for something. When asked what he was seeking, he replied, "A man."

He wasn't looking for immaturity in a grown body given to child's play. He sought character qualities— a person strong in conviction, unyielding in purpose, brave in heart, honest to the core, dependable through and through, good from head to toe.

The world is still looking for that kind of character in men and women in multiplied millions— and each one of us can be one of them!

*Nearly all people can stand adversity, but if you want to test a person's character, give him power.*

— Anonymous

*When I became a man,*
*I put away childish things.*
— I Corinthians 13:11

# IMAGINARY TROUBLES

There are enough real troubles without imagining some. Many people are suffering from hurts which are only figmental, but that makes the pain no less. We shall have more energy and poise to face real adversities, if we don't tire ourselves with conceived ones.

Carved over a mantel in an old farm house was Mark Twain's summation of troubles: "I am an old man and have known a great many troubles, but most of them never happened." This reflection gave hope to the farmer who ever had to face the possibility of floods, droughts, storms, breakdowns and insects.

*Some of your hurts you have cured,*
*And the sharpest you still have survived,*
*But what torments of grief you endured*
*From the evil which never arrived.*
— Ralph Waldo Emerson
1803-1882

*O Lord, You preserve man and beast.*
— Psalm 36:6

# LAUGH A LITTLE

*T*here is a time to laugh; and when the time comes, don't miss it. We must learn to express ourselves in joy. Laughter is a victory over a world of ills that plague humanity. And when we can laugh at ourselves, that is some victory— we have become an adult.

Laughter is good medicine for relieving the strain of life, loosening tight nerves, and increasing strength for the performance of duties, and it is more enjoyable than the pharmaceutical kind. Another thing— it will keep us from being a bore!

*Laughter is God's hand on a troubled world.*

— Anonymous

*To every thing there is a season,*
*and a time to every purpose under the heaven:*
*. . .a time to weep and a time to laugh. . .*
— Ecclesiastes 3:1-4

# IMMORTALITY IS REASONABLE

It adds zest to this life to hope for another life. It gives more today because we believe there shall be more tomorrow— eternal life.

If there is not another life, then why this one? Animal life and vegetable life exist for the benefit of mankind; and if we be lost, forever lost, all of nature fails. Animals are born and die. Vegetation springs out of the earth and returns. Now if we live on the same level— live and die never to live again then nature labors and toils to no permanent accomplishment, and the plan of the universe is a hopeless and colossal failure.

*The ancient heavens will roll aside for me,*
*As Moses monarch'd the dividing sea.*
*This body is my house— it is not I.*
*Triumphant in this faith I live, and die.*
— Frederic Lawrence Knowles

*And this is the promise that He*
*has promised us— eternal life.*
— I John 2:25

# DESIGNED FOR IMMORTALITY

We never would have been fashioned as we are, if it had not been meant for us to be immortal. Surely we would not have been endowed with such hopes just to have them crushed. We who were created with the ability to triumph over every obstacle, to fly with the birds, and to traverse the planets, surely were designed to take wings and triumph over death.

If we are not immortal, then we are completely inexplicable; for it wouldn't make sense for us to live like humans and die like dogs. Thus our very nature is such that immortality is too necessary not to be true.

*Dust thou art, to dust returneth,*
*Was not spoken of the soul.*
— Henry Wadsworth Longfellow
1807-1882

*Then the dust will return to the earth as it was:*
*and the spirit will return to God who gave it.*
—Ecclesiastes 12:7

*April 3*

# A NEW EDITION

*O*ur only hope of permanence is found in our dual nature— flesh and spirit. This enables us to lay aside the corruptible body for an incorruptible one suited to an everlasting habitation.

I have stood in the old cemetery of Christ Church, Philadelphia, at the grave of one of the world's brightest and most versatile geniuses— Benjamin Franklin. As I stood there in appreciation of him and in examination of my soul, I reflected upon the epitaph he composed for his own tomb:

*Like the cover of an old book,*
*Its contents torn out,*
*And stripped of its lettering and gilding,*
*Lies here food for worms;*
*But the work shall not be lost,*
*For it will (as he believes) appear once more*
*In a new and more elegant edition,*
*Revised and corrected by the Author.*
— Benjamin Franklin
1706 -1790

*For this corruptible must put on incorruption,*
*and this mortal must put on immortality.*
— I Corinthians 15:53

*April 4*

# EVERY LEAF OF SPRINGTIME

*T*he resurrection of man is just as reasonable as the resurrection of nature. The cold, harsh wintry winds which seem opposed to us sweep down from the frozen North, biting and chilling all nature, stripping the trees of their foliage, turning the grass into the color of death. But they later return as gentle breezes in friendly fashion from the warm South land, resurrecting all sleeping vegetation into a more beautiful life.

Surely mankind, the crowning glory of creation, shall fare as well as a vegetable! Surely the Creator who has the power to resurrect nature shall not fail to use that power on us!

*Our Lord has written the promise of resurrection,*
*not in books alone, but in every leaf in springtime.*
— Martin Luther
1484-1546


*I am the resurrection, and the life.*
*He who believes in Me,*
*though he die, he shall live.*
— John 11:25

*April 5*

# DEATH PROVIDES TRANSITION

It is especially fitting that at this time of year we reflect upon the resurrection; for apart from our resurrection there is no abiding purpose in life and no eternal hope in death.

Our immortal nature accentuates our transitive state. Our birth was our entrance into this world; our living here is our schooling; and our death shall be our exit from it and our entrance into another one.

So death has its kindlier aspects. It was designed as gain: to bring relief to pain, to stop the flow of tears, to shorten the days of trial, to bid the soul go free.

*Death is not the journey into an unknown land; it is a voyage home. We are going not to a strange country, but to our Father's house, and among our kith and kin.*
— John Ruskin
1819-1900

*And it came to pass,
as her soul was in departing,
(for she died).*
— Genesis 35:18

# PILGRIMS

We are sustained in the belief that we are pilgrims passing through this earth to another shore where loved ones await our arrival.

*I am standing upon the seashore.*
*A ship at my side spreads her white sails*
*to the morning breeze and starts for the blue ocean. . .*
*I stand and watch her until at length she hangs*
*like a speck of white cloud come down to mingle*
*with each other. Then someone at my side says,*
*"There! She's gone!"*

*Gone where? Gone from my sight. . . that is all.*
*She is just as large in mast and hull and spar*
*as she was when she left my side. . .*
*Her diminished size is in me, not in her.*
*And just at the moment when someone at my side says,*
*"There! She's gone!"— there are other eyes*
*watching her coming, and other voices ready*
*to take up the glad shout, "There she comes!"*
*And that is dying.*

— Anonymous

*Man goes to his long home,*
*and the mourners go about the streets.*
— Ecclesiastes 12:5

# ON BENDED KNEE

If "In God we trust," then we trust in prayer. Prayer gives strength in weakness, courage in despair. It is the shield which protects from the blows and darts of an inconsiderate world. It is the bed upon which frailty sleeps in peace, and where worry has lost its power to vex.

So when you feel weak, drop to your knees— in prayer. There our burdens will not press us to stumble; there our tired souls can rest; there we can reverently address our needs to a Greater Power. Of course, for our words to get through, we should not live too far away.

*I have been driven many times to my knees*
*by the overwhelming conviction that I had*
*nowhere else to go. My own wisdom and that*
*of all about me seemed insufficient for the day.*
— Abraham Lincoln
1809-1865

*And when He had sent the multitude away,*
*He went up on a mountain by Himself to pray.*
*And when evening had come,*
*He was alone there.*
— Matthew 14:23

*April 8*

# TAKE IT STRAIGHT

We should not read anything into the Good Book, if we wish to get anything out of it— just take it straight. Instead of trying to alter our Bibles to fit us, we must change ourselves to fit it; otherwise we will have God's transformation process in reverse.

What we think of the Bible does not affect it— just us. If it appears too deep, we surely need the exercise it affords to think deeper. If it looks too exacting, we definitely require its influence to keep from straying. And if it seems dry, it might be that we have allowed too much dust to accumulate on it.

*I am profitably engaged in reading the Bible.*
*Take all of this book upon reason that you can*
*and the balance upon faith,*
*and you will live and die a better man.*
— Abraham Lincoln
1809-1865

*You shall not add to the word which I command you,*
*nor take anything from it.*
— Deuteronomy 4:2

# BETTER IN BIG DOSES

*R*eligion to some people is like a person with a headache. He does not want to get rid of his head, but oh! how it hurts him to keep it! They have enough faith to make them miserable, but not enough to make them happy. The chief danger to religion is our wanting it in such small amounts. Religion is better in big doses.

We enjoy what we work at, and in religion there is no joy apart from a working faith. By putting our heart into it and working at the job, we find the indispensable support of ideals, sense of purpose, peace, approval, hope and joy.

*The religion of some people is constrained:*
*they are like people who use the cold bath. . .*
*they go in with reluctance,*
*and are glad when they get out.*
— John Newton
1725-1807

*If anyone among you thinks he is religious . . .*
*but deceives himself and his religion is worthless.*
— James 1:26

*April 10*

# DEEPER THAN SKIN

*W*hy care I for the beautiful brown shell of the pecan or walnut, if it is worm-eaten? About the only purpose it serves is to emphasize a difference between superficiality and reality, outward beauty and inward beauty.

Sooner or later our own appetite will settle for nothing less than the real meat of goodness, for the world can't live on empty shells and barren husks.

Physical beauty is only the framework, walls, paint and adornments, which nature displays outside the house, but what about the host or hostess who dwells within? What does he or she look like? The beauty that is deeper than skin is the only real beauty.

*Though we travel the world over to find the beautiful, we must carry it within us, or we find it not.*
— Ralph Waldow Emerson
1803-1882

*And she was a woman of good understanding and beautiful appearance.*
— I Samuel 25:3

*April 11*

# BIGGER VALUES

*L*ife has its greatest charm when we give ourselves to some person or cause we value above self. Only in the pursuit of such love and conviction can we find peace and satisfaction. It increases our grip on life and impels us to more vigorous living, without which the days are dull and boring.

The animal lives on the level where survival is the major consideration, but to the highest type of person there are other matters more important.

Some find the bigger values in such areas as relationship with God, love for others, loyalty to country and a good name. For these they are willing to die rather than compromise.

*Learn to hold loosely all that is not eternal.*
— Agnes Royden
1876-1956

*Nor do I count my life dear to myself.*
— Acts 20:24

# WHEN THERE ARE TEARS

Tears are a universal language. They often tell what words will not express. Sincerely shed, they are not willing water from a handy hydrant to be turned on and off at will, but rather the natural droplets from a heart too full to be contained. Tears are the language of the heart, and where there is a heart, there can be a tear.

Watery eyes have been known to see what clear eyes could not detect. When our plight seems so hopeless that we can't see our way through, take another look through our tears. They may prove to be telescopic.

*If you have tears, prepare to shed them now.*
— William Shakespeare
1564-1616

*They that sow in tears shall reap in joy.*
— Psalm 126:5

# DRIFTWOOD OR AN OAK?

What are our purposes or plans for life? To be a piece of driftwood or a towering oak? Drifters float on chance, and the stream gets more perilous by the moment.

We must put purpose in our lives. Be resolute. Never submit to passiveness. Drifting is dangerous. For the course of least resistance always points downstream.

It takes a strong purpose and a strong muscle to make it upstream. The only way is to lift the anchor and grab an oar, and still better— two oars. We will make our share of mistakes, but we won't make the one of doing nothing.

*Great minds have purposes, others have wishes.*
— Washington Irving
1783-1859

*So let each one give as he purposes in his heart. . . .*
— II Corinthians 9:7

# WORRY NOT

$\mathcal{B}$e concerned, but not worried. Be warm enough to have interest, but cool enough to be calm.

Fretting never solves problems— it creates more. Worry puts fuzziness in our head, a knot in our stomach and a pack on our back. Nothing is as hurtful as worry; nothing as helpful as concern. Indifference never sees the problems; worry tangles them; but concern unravels them.

We must be enterprising enough to do our best and trustful enough to leave it with God. Do all we can and then do a little more by not worrying. Mortals can do no more than this.

*Worry is an indication that we think*
*God cannot look after us.*
— Oswald Chambers
1874-1917

# WAKE UP

Wake up! The good life comes to those who are awake enough to see and hear and move.

No person has ever yawned his way to greatness. The sleeper sleeps through his opportunities. And while he slumbers, his talents sleep with him. And while asleep, he remains down.

Sometimes the moon appears hazy and sleepy, but it is more beautiful and more useful when wide awake— and so are we. No one ever just woke up and found himself great or successful or anything else worth desiring. You may not have heard of him before, but he's been awake the whole time.

*To be awake is to be alive.*
— Henry David Thoreau
1817-1862

*Awake, you who sleep,*
*arise from the dead.*
— Ephesians 5:14

April 16

# IT BELONGS TO THE FREE

Who can call today his own? Only the free. But not every one is free whom the law says is free. Regardless of the statute books, the only free person is the one whose heart is unfettered. Unshackled within, they have the freest freedom without. They are not hindered by hate, fettered by fear, curbed by conscience, or daunted by doubt. Today is his, because he is his. To him the fast-breaking day comes unrestrained because he has the freedom to receive it.

Thus, it is not the tick of the clock that gives us today—it is the beat of the heart.

*Happy the man, and happy he alone,*
*Who can call today his own;*
*He who, secure within, can say,*
*"Tomorrow, do thy worst, for I have lived today."*

— John Dryden
1631-1700

*See, I have set before you today life and good,*
*death and evil.*

— Deuteronomy 30:15

# GET UNDERSTANDING

*I*t is dangerous to drive in a fog, especially if it's a mental fog. We must be aware of what's going on around us. When we don't understand, search deeper, look longer, consult others, think, analyze, reach logical conclusions. Clarity makes the wise wiser and the safe safer.

Being misunderstood by others is not half as bad as not understanding others. What we need most, perhaps, is comprehension. No one is prepared to make intelligent decisions about matters he doesn't understand. No person can do better than he knows. Only as we begin to understand can we figure out things. Without knowledge our decisions are only blind guesses.

*O God, help us not to despise*
*or oppose what we do not understand.*
— William Penn
1644-1718

*Discretion will preserve you;*
*understanding will keep you.*
— Proverbs 2:11

# BLESSED BY TEMPTATION

*H*uman beings are equated to weakness— some more than others, but there is a frailty in us all. This implies that each one must ever be on the guard against temptation, which when faced and overcome makes us stronger. But when not resisted, makes us that much weaker.

Hence, every temptation presents an opportunity to acquire strength and virtue— if we prevail. If there were no temptations in the world, there could be no attainment through testing and there could be no valid claim to virtue. Beyond question, those who struggle and win prove themselves conquerors.

*Unless there is within us that which is above us,*
*we shall soon yield to that which is about us.*
— P.T. Forsyth
1803-1882


*Blessed is the man who endures temptation;*
*for when he has been proved, he will receive the crown of life*
*which the Lord has promised to those who love Him.*
— James 1:12

*April 19*

# TIME CHANGES THINGS

Only time can solve some of our troubles. Whatever we offer as today's solution is resisted. But tomorrow it shall be different. As time changes the calendar, it changes circumstances. Time is an ointment for bleeding hearts, an arbitrator for dissolved friendships, a restorer of broken health and a regainer of lost fortune. Time has the power to dry tears, steady nerves, renew courage, lift eyes.

Time sees to it that the winter passes and spring bursts anew.

What a powerful and hopeful lesson the calendar teaches! And as long as it keeps turning for us, there is hope.

*Time is a precious gift of God; so precious that he only gives it to us moment by moment.*

— Amelia Barr
1831-1919


*Lord, let it alone this year also,*
*until I dig about it .*

— Luke 13:8

# THE CHEERFUL

e can attract more people with cheerfulness than with gloom.

Most of us feel the end will come soon enough without having doomsday peddlers trying to clothe us in verbal shrouds before our time.

We prefer the people who light up rooms when they walk in. How eagerly we gather around them. Such is the wondrous and magnetic power of cheerfulness. The happy person is a welcome ray of gladness to this shadow-cast and troubled world. Needy humanity craves the presence of the person who lightens burdens, mitigates misfortunes, scatters clouds, and looks to the dawn when the night is the darkest.

We can all be the cheerful person others seek. Let us rejoice and be glad.

*Cheerfulness keeps up a kind of daylight in the mind,
and fills it with a steady and perpetual serenity.*

— Joseph Addison
1672-1719

*This is the day which the Lord has made;
we will rejoice and be glad.*

— Psalm 118:24

# BE WHAT YOU ARE

he world is a stage where each is cast to play his own role, and the plaudits and encores are for only the ones who do. Sooner or later it is curtains for the imitators. The audience can't be fooled long. They are quick to spot a phony. When he opens his mouth he sounds like an amateur actor. He's unreal.

In the drama of life, theatrics are out of order. The stage is actual; the audience is genuine; and play actors are not tolerated. We must be ourselves. But we should be such a self that we feel no need to act another.

*Be not imitator; freshly act thy part;*
*Through this world be thou an independent ranger;*
*Better is the faith that springeth from thy heart*
*Than a better faith belonging to a stranger.*
— From the Persian

*And God said unto Moses,*
*I AM THAT I AM.*
— Exodus 3:14

*April 22*

# A GOOD LISTENER

*T*he great majority of us value listening, especially if someone else is doing it. Just listening to a person is enough for him to regard us as a friend. With dull, cold ears it is impossible to warm the heart of another. A hearing ear makes more friends than a wagging tongue.

Some places we go we have to pay to listen; but the everyday run of people will pay us to listen to them. They will pay us in appreciation, popularity, kindness, and some even in wisdom. We can make a swap: give them our ears, and they will give us their hearts, their praises, their purses and additionally, some knowledge.

*A good listener is not only popular everywhere,*
*but after a while he knows something.*
— Wilson Mizner

*Let every man be swift to hear,*
*slow to speak, slow to wrath.*
— James 1:19

# ROSES IN DECEMBER

It takes years to grow an oak— and men and women. Both lumber and brains season with time.

Deep rivers have had the flow of many waters, and deep minds have had the passing of many thoughts.

Most of the great people of history distinguished themselves after fifty. Distinction requires more than impulsive action— guided movement. It requires more than high speed— direction.

The University of Hard Knocks has its lessons; they are hard, but effective. The price of getting wiser is getting older— plus getting a few bumps and bruises. Years should teach, and— if one is a good student— they will.

*God gave us memories*
*that we might have roses in December.*
— James M. Barrier
1860-1937


*I said, "Age should speak,*
*and multitude of years should teach wisdom."*
— Job 32:7

*April 24*

# THE FAMILY TREE AND ME

*We* can never make a place for ourselves in the sun, if we continually take refuge in the shade of the family tree.

No doubt the tree has had some distinctive limbs— we won't say anything about the shoddy ones— but what I need to do is to decide to be the best branch on it and start growing toward the sun. I shouldn't make a camp ground of where some dead limbs fell.

Today makes no demands of my forefathers; it rather asks: what am I doing? They lived their lives— now it is my turn.

*I don't know who my grandfather was;*
*I am much more concerned to know*
*what his grandson will be.*
— Abraham Lincoln
1809 -1865

*But avoid foolish disputes, genealogies,*
*contentions, and strivings about the law;*
*for they are unprofitable and useless.*
— Titus 3:9

# JUST ENOUGH OBSTACLES

A touch of difficulty gives a little muscle to life—provided we have the backbone to meet it. Humility is encouraged. Self-reliance is taught. Patience is required. Inventiveness is urged. Many unknown and hidden powers buried deep in the soul are called up. And when the trouble is whipped, that day belongs to the conqueror.

Paul, the apostle, had a thorn in the flesh, and so does everybody else; the difference being in the kind, the size and the sharpness. But whatever our particular thorn is, it can be our hidden blessing.

Blessed are those who have just enough obstacles.

*Many men owe the grandeur of their lives*
*to their tremendous difficulties.*
— Charles Haddon Spurgeon
1834-1892

*But He knows the way that I take:*
*when He has tested me,*
*I shall come forth as gold.*
— Job 23:10

*April 26*

# SWAPPING SHOES

*T*here are some who limp, but very few out of choice. The majority have cause. And the face shows what the feet feel.

Before we criticize the limper, we should try his shoes. It might give us an education no university can provide and a feeling no sermon can effect.

The faultfinder would be more tolerant of another's limp, if he had to wear for a little while those nail-piercing shoes the other fellow has to wear all the time. What a change in tone and pace, if society were to swap shoes. Faces which now smile would have their tears.

*Happy the man who could search out*
*the cause of things.*
— Virgil
70-19 B.C.

*What have I now done?*
*Is there not a cause?*
— I Samuel 17:29

# FILLING EMPTY HEARTS

At times all of us are lonely. It brings an emptiness within. A feeling of inadequacy and a lack of direction overwhelm us. We should not, however, allow loneliness to cheat us out of a single day. And here are some ways we can all overcome it:

- Like yourself enough that you can be happy alone
- As a pilgrim, know your map
- Have something to do and do it
- Make good books interesting companions
- Pull down any selfish walls you may have built around yourself
- Make your presence desired, and the best way to do this is to find emptier hearts and fill them with love

*Seldom can the heart be lonely,*
*If it seeks a lonelier still;*
*Self-forgetting, seeking only*
*Emptier cups of love to fill.*
— Frances R. Havergal

*I alone am left.*
— I Kings 19:10

# THE MUD WON'T MATTER

*T*he slander others say about us is not as damaging as any evil we might vindictively say about them. Speaking evil of another hurts the defamer more than the defamed. There is always a certain amount of sympathy for the attacked— innocent or guilty— but for the attacker, never!

If we maintain clean hands and a pure heart, the other person's mud won't matter; it is not going to hurt us very much. But what about him? Not only will the world see his soiled hands, but it will sooner or later decide that it heard only a croaking frog in a muddy pond.

*Don't soil your hands by slinging mud.*
— Anonymous

*And Saul lifted up his voice, and wept.*
*Then he said to David: "You are more righteous than I;*
*for you have rewarded me with good,*
*whereas I have rewarded you with evil."*
— I Samuel 24:16, 17

*April 29*

# FRESH HEAT

*E*nvy is fresh heat from torment. It blisters itself with its own perverted thermology; it makes itself miserable with its own miseries; it sorrows because it cannot rejoice in another's fortune.

Envy is negative and destructive. Discontentment because of what others have will not add to our possessions. There is, however, greatness in climbing on our own virtues— not in seeing others depressed to our level.

Be stirred with love— not envy. Be too big to begrudge, too good to be dissatisfied with your neighbor's prosperity.

Furthermore, outward appearances are too deceptive for us to envy anybody.

> *If every man's internal care*
> *Were written on his brow,*
> *How many would our pity share*
> *Who raise our envy now?*
> — Pietro Metastasio

> *Again, I saw that for all toil and every skillful work*
> *a man is envied by his neighbor.*
> *This also is vanity and grasping for the wind.*
> — Ecclesiastes 4:4

*April 30*

# KEEPING SCORE

Looking to find fault is dangerous, for we all have them. It is a game two can play and the other person may come up with the highest score, find more in us than we find in him.

If we knock the other person, his door won't open to us; neither will his neighbor's. Those doors swing on hinges of toleration.

The world will be more responsive if we have a good word for everybody, for those above us and for those below us. The ones above us deserve it, and the ones below us— well, even the tombstones praise those beneath them.

*There is so much good in the worst of us,*
*and so much bad in the best of us,*
*that it hardly behooves any of us*
*to talk about the rest of us.*
— Edward Hoch

*They found fault.*
— Mark 7:2

## QUEST

We often hear there is a pot of gold at the end of the rainbow. What we rarely hear is how few find it. Furthermore, we seldom hear the conditions for finding it: that we must travel the distance to it and then dig, and in most cases, again and again. The rainbow is ours for the seeing, but the gold— now that is different— it is ours only through quest.

It is a joy to gaze at the rainbow, but if we want the gold at its base start searching— and don't forget to carry the pick. The best in life is for only the seekers!

*There are deep things of God,*
*Push out from shore;*
*Hast thou found much?*
*Give thanks, and look for more.*
— Charles Gordon Ames

*The land which we passed through to spy out*
*is an exceedingly good land.*
— Numbers 14:7

*May 2*

# ACTION!

*S*uccess requires action. The way to better ourselves is to get started. A moving object has more force than a stationary one. When a person rises from a sitting position, he doubles the force of his pressure on the ground. While standing still, his pressure is minimum, because it is downward; but on moving, he exerts a side force greater than his weight.

This illustrates mankind's force in other areas. In sitting (idleness), his power is very little. In arising (making a beginning), he doubles his force. In moving (doing something), he multiplies his force many times.

*Every action of our lives touches on some chord*
*that will vibrate in eternity.*
— Edwin Chapin
1814-1880

*The man Jeroboam was a mighty man of valor;*
*and Solomon, seeing that the young man was*
*industrious, made him the officer over all the labor*
*force of the house of Joseph.*
— I Kings 11:28

*May 3*

# NOW IS THE TIME

A farmer once lay desperately ill in a hospital. For weeks he struggled between life and death, much of the time in a coma. One morning he regained consciousness and asked his nurse what time it was. She replied, "It is springtime, and nature is bursting forth with renewed vigor."

"Springtime," said the patient. "Then I can't die now, for it is time to plow."

For all of us, now is plowing time. The only time to which we are joined is now. With this attitude, today can be mine; and so can tomorrow when it becomes today.

*Now or never was the time.*
— Laurence Sterne
1713-1768

*And now, Lord, what do I wait for?*
— Psalm 39:7

*May 4*

# DON'T STOP FOR THE DOGS

*W*hen I was a boy, we occasionally traveled the country roads into town. Dogs would run out and bark at us, but my father said that if we stopped to chase them off, we never would get to town. Reaching our destination was more important than chasing dogs.

When we have a goal to reach, pursue it. When we have a work to do, do it. Be not deterred by criticism nor any other diversion.

It takes the will to continue to get there. There is no magic that will turn the trick. It is all a matter of concentration and grit.

> *I go through my appointed daily stage,*
> *and I care not for the dogs*
> *who bark at me along the road.*
> — Frederick the Great
> 1712-1786

> *Turn not to the right hand nor to the left.*
> — Proverbs 4:27

*May 5*

# SPEAK AND LET SPEAK

Time about is fair play, even when it comes to speaking and listening. We can't expect others to listen to us if we are unwilling to listen to them.

It is difficult to listen to what we don't believe, but maybe the other fellow has the same problem when he listens to us.

Speak and let speak grants freedom of speech to all. It takes bigness on the inside to give others a respectful hearing when they express views contrary to ours. Naturally, every one likes to hear the smart people who agree with him, but this is no test of magnanimity at all.

*I do not agree with a word you say,*
*but I will defend to the death your right to say it.*
— Francois Marie Aroult Voltaire
1694-1778

*And some said, "What does this babbler want to say?"*
*And they took him, and brought him to the Areopagus,*
*saying, "May we know what this new doctrine*
*is of which you speak?"*
— Acts 17:18,19

# THE FAMILY FORTRESS

Home? What is it? It is the word that strikes melody in the heart. It is something we associate with mother. It is the place of rest to which the care-worn soul turns tired steps from the toils and struggles of life. It is the family fortress that shuts out the world. It is where the weak and weary spirit finds strength. It is the one place in this wide world where hearts are sure of each other. It is the only place where the commoner can be a king or a queen or a prince or a princess.

We call it Home, Sweet Home.

*What is home without a mother?*
— Alice Hawthorne

*She watches over the ways
of her household.*
— Proverbs 31:27

## *May 7*

# HOME IS WHERE MOTHER IS

*A* child was asked, "Where is your home?" The little girl replied, "Where mother is." Ah, this is home!

She has been endowed with special feminine and gracious traits which nobly qualify her for the strenuous and honorable task of being a homemaker. What night-watching! what self-denial! what tears! what concern! what joy! what helpfulness is seen in the home mother makes! She forges the ties of an undying love and welds the bonds of a family trust as she makes them proud in their poverty, sincere in their simplicity and one in their plurality.

This is home. And this is bliss.

> *There are three words that sweetly blend,*
> *And on the heart are graven.*
> *A precious, soothing balm they lend,*
> *They're "Mother," "Home," and "Heaven."*
> — Anonymous

> *To be discreet, chaste, homemakers. . .*
> — Titus 2:5

# HER GREATEST ROLE

The greatest mission of woman is motherhood. In this eminent calling she glorifies the Creator and perpetuates His creation.

It is a task that involves a thousand sacrifices, but womanhood with a song on her lips and a prayer in her heart rises triumphantly. At travail of body and anxiety of mind, she makes human life possible. And then, little by little, she gives her life to see this new life blossom into noble maturity.

As she shapes the character of her children, she shapes the destiny of nations. Upon her role all future progress depends.

*Who fed me from her gentle breast*
*And hushed me in her arms to rest,*
*And on my cheek sweet kisses prest?*
*My mother.*

— Jane Taylor
1783-1824

*And Adam called his wife's name Eve;*
*because she was the mother of all living.*

— Genesis 3:20

*May 9*

# A MOTHER'S WORK

A mother works and works and works. And the willingness with which she does it is the chief contribution to a pleasant and happy family.

It has been said that the thrush goes to work at half-past two every morning during the summer and works until nine-thirty at night— a straight nineteen hours— during which it feeds its young over two hundred times.

The blackbird works seventeen hours and feeds its little ones a hundred times a day.

In the home the energetic mother is up early and retires late. Like the hard-working bird, she does it for those who are so precious to her.

*A man's work is from sun to sun,*
*But a mother's work is never done.*
— Anonymous

*She also rises while it is yet night,*
*and provides food for her household,*
*and a portion for her maidens.*
— Proverbs 31:15

# MOTHER'S ROCKING CHAIR

Let me tell you about an old chair that symbolizes greatness in child training. It was mother's rocking chair. It had to have rockers because she had so many cares and troubles to soothe.

There the children sobbed out their hurts and worries. There advice was given. There character was developed. There nobler aspirations were born. There sympathy was extended. There assurance held sway. There sleep was more inviting than in bed.

It was a combination nursery, pulpit, classroom, lecture hall, library and study room. Whatever it was, we desperately need it today, squeak and all, for even the squeak was music— music to the heart.

*Earth's finest school— mother was instructor there!*
*Oh! the learning that came from her old rocking chair!*
— Anonymous

*Forsake not the law of thy mother.*
— Proverbs 6:20

# MOTHER-MADE

To a large extent we are mother-made. She instills a way of life in the little heart. She throws a spell around the child which is hard to break. Years later the child is apt to mirror the mother.

At a great meeting of prominent women, one was introduced as a "self-made woman." Instead of enjoying the tribute, she seemed to be bothered by it. For a few moments, she appeared to be in a deep study. Then she broke the silence by saying, "No, I am not a 'self-made woman.' I think my mother had much to do with it."

And right she was!

*The mother's heart is the child's schoolroom.*
— Henry Ward Beecher
1813-1887

*As is the mother, so is her daughter.*
— Ezekiel 16:44

*May 12*

# MY ANGEL MOTHER

*O*f all the human names held sacred in our memory, none equals the sweet and sublime name of mother. How precious in after years are the recollections of a mother's patient training. How many have nobly ascribed all recognized success to the devotion and guidance of mother. Through helpless infancy her throbbing heart was our strong support and safe protection.

It is not strange, therefore, that we feel animated to struggle more courageously in life's great battle when we recall mother's prayers in childhood's early dawn, and think upon her counsels in youth's slippery path. Those lofty precepts! Impressions as durable as time!

> *All that I am or hope to be,*
> *I owe to my angel mother.*
> — Abraham Lincoln
> 1809-1865

> *Her children rise up*
> *and call her blessed.*
> — Proverbs 31:28

## May 13

# LOVE'S FIRES

*L*ove turns on the sun and exclaims, "All is well with the world!"

Only love brings out our full size. It discovers within us ambitions unnumbered and goodness unlimited. It multiplies an energy way beyond our imagination and keeps us going long after others drop. It excites a courage braver than any soldier and stands us up to face bombs and bullets, scandal and shame.

It comforts like warm sunshine, refreshes like gentle rain.

Love's fires always glow the longest; its arrows are the sharpest; its tender kisses are the sweetest; its hours are the shortest.

It speaks and hears a language known only to lovers. And blessed are those who find it.

*Love is like a friendship caught on fire.*
*In the beginning a flame, very pretty, often hot and fierce*
*but still only light and flickering. As love grows older,*
*our hearts mature and our love becomes as coals,*
*deep-burning and unquenchable.*

— Bruce Lee

*His banner over me was love.*

— Song of Solomon 2:4

*May 14*

# CONSCIENCE AFFECTS BRAVERY

An unafraid conscience is a great contributor to courage. Bravery for life's struggles requires scrupulous living. A condemning self is tuned to every fright, for it thinks others know. But with no skeletons hanging in the heart, we feel no need to run. Knowing that we have nothing to hide, we can eyeball every one.

For a stronger, braver and more fearless life, live on the approving side of conscience. Be confident your cause is just; be certain you believe in what you do; be sure you treat the other person right; and therein you shall find courage to stand.

*Thus conscience does make cowards of us all.*
— William Shakespeare
1564-1616

*The wicked flee when no one pursues,*
*but the righteous are bold as a lion.*
— Proverbs 28:1

# BE OF GOOD COURAGE

*O*ur times demand courage. For a great society cannot sprout from weaklings. Nor a well managed world from ill managed lives. We need men and women who can stand up to the world, remake it, reshape it.

The person of courage is the can, the will, the does, the won't. He can stand, he will stand, he does stand, he won't back off.

But the weakling doesn't have the strength for the clash. He is bent and broken when the world hits him. She doesn't have the strength to meet the pressures with a strong force. They lose. And their loss is the world's loss.

*Take courage. We walk in the wilderness today and in the Promised Land tomorrow.*
— Dwight L. Moody
1837-1899

*Be of good courage, and let us be strong for our people.*
— II Samuel 10:12

# DON'T TROUBLE TROUBLE

*A* good way to stay out of trouble is not to trouble trouble until trouble troubles you. Don't ask for it.

We are of few days and full of trouble, but our troubles will be fewer and our days happier if we mind our own business. If we keep quiet, there is a good chance trouble will pass us by.

The troublemaker is usually in trouble because he or she has a genius for getting into it. But the peacemakers are ordinarily at peace because they have a talent for proceeding softly where conflict may break loose. They know it is good to let a sleeping dog lie.

*First keep the peace within yourself,*
*then you can also bring peace to others.*
— Thomas À Kempis
1380-1471

*He who passes by and meddles in a quarrel not*
*his own is like one who takes a dog by the ears.*
— Proverbs 26:17

*May 17*

# DON'T LISTEN TO THEM

Today is mine provided I am ready to appropriate it. If my outlook is not prepared for today, then today is not mine— except to breathe, and that's not enough to make it mine. To capitalize today, I must not listen to those who tell me I'm too young or too old to accomplish my goals and dreams.

> *When I was seventeen I heard*
> *From each censorious tongue,*
> *"I'd not do that if I were you;*
> *You see you're rather young."*
>
> *Now that I number forty years,*
> *I'm quite as often told*
> *Of this or that I shouldn't do*
> *Because I'm quite too old.*
>
> *O carping world! If there's an age*
> *Where youth and manhood keep*
> *An equal poise, alas! I must*
> *Have passed it in my sleep.*
> — Walter Learned

*And Saul said to David, "You are not able to go against this Philistine to fight with him; for you are but a youth, and he a man of war from his youth."*
— I Samuel 17:33

# RIGHT FOR RIGHT'S SAKE

It takes all kinds to make a world, but there are enough other people— without us— to contribute the wrongs. And the darker they make the world, the brighter you can shine.

Do right for the sake of right, for there is reward enough in the virtue of doing it.

In the struggle between good and bad, we should look not at how the world is lining up, but rather at how right and wrong are shaping up. Let that determine our course. And then so follow it that we can say each night, "I am glad this day I have done the right."

*Do right, and God's reward to you*
*will be power to do more right.*
— Frederick Robertson
1816-1853

*And he did what was right*
*in the sight of the Lord.*
— II Kings 14:3

# THE PRETENDER

Pretending doesn't make sense. It's make-believe, play-acting, fakery, humbuggery. If the world is real— and it is— then there is no place for sham.

Hypocrisy may look good, but it's only a wolf in sheep's clothing; sounds good, but it never intends to keep its promises; appears good, but it's merely trying to cash in on goodness. It's bad! bad because it's a sham! A fraud that solely thinks of self!

Hypocrisy makes one only a performer. The word without the heart is still unspoken— just feigned. The deed without the doer still remains undone— just acted.

If we are anything, let us be real.

*You may charge me with murder—*
*or want of sense—*
*(We are all of us weak at times):*
*But the slightest approach to a false pretense*
*Was never among my crimes!*
— Lewis Carroll
1832-1898

*For the vile person will speak villainy,*
*and his heart will work iniquity,*
*to practice hypocrisy.*
— Isaiah 32:6

*May 20*

# THE FAULTFINDER

*N*o statue has ever been set up to a faultfinder. Our two main objections to him is he has eyes and ears which see and hear our faults bigger than they are, and then puts a tongue in this sin of his.

There is a difference in fact-finding and faultfinding. The fact-finder sees good just as freely as evil. But the faultfinder is biased in favor of the faults. That is about all he can see.

Humanity is imperfect. But in most people there is much more good than bad. Take a white sheet of paper and make a blotch in the center of it. What do you see? A spot. But think how much more whiteness there is around it.

*Man judges from a partial view*
*None ever yet his brother knew.*
— John Greenleaf Whittier
1807-1892

*But with me it is a very small thing*
*that I should be judged*
*by you or by a human court.*
*In fact, I do not even judge myself.*
— I Corinthians 4:3

# HANDLE WITH CARE

If circumstances suggest we mention to another his faults, let us put ourselves in his place before we start. Consider your own imperfections.

Remember— the offender's heart is fragile, handle it with care.

Be not a hindrance but a help. Do it not for vengeance, but for virtue. Hasten to heal, don't rush to retort. Be firm but fair, pointed but patient, censorious but considerate. Be gentle. Be kind.

And if our message should be rejected, at least our manners will have to be admired. And the assurance that we have done right, in the right way, will give us a softer pillow for sweeter sleep.

*Deal with the faults of others*
*as gently as with your own.*
— Confucius
551-479 B.C.

*But the wisdom that is from above*
*is first pure, then peaceable, gentle,*
*willing to yield, full of mercy and good fruits,*
*without partiality and without hypocrisy.*
— James 3:17

# BIGGER THAN THE OBSTACLE

*T*he point of disappointment is to learn not a bitter but better way.

You can tell the size of a person by how much it takes to stop him or her. By climbing over the rubbish of disappointment, they prove themselves bigger than the obstacle.

Accept disappointments hopefully. For some are inevitable. There always have been some clouds without moisture, some rivers without water, and some expectations without realization. But never quit! Never turn sour! There is always cause for hope. Just as the sun goes down every night, it also rises every morning. We must reshuffle our plans and keep on striving.

*Disappointment is often the salt of life.*
— Theodore Parker
1810-1860

*You looked for much,*
*but indeed it came to little.*
— Haggai 1:9

# THE DIVIDENDS OF GOODNESS

We— like the bee that seeks honey or the vulture that seeks carrion— find what we seek; and what we seek finds us. Whatever we draw near to meets us, and whatever we flee from flees from us. This is why so much good comes to some people. The returns. The dividends on the investment.

Doing good sooner or later returns to its source. Full measure and running over. So instead of thinking so much about receiving good, it is better to get busy and do good and let the receiving take care of itself.

*Goodness is the only investment that never fails.*
— Henry David Thoreau
1817-1862

*He who follows righteousness and mercy*
*finds life, righteousness and honor.*
— Proverbs 21:21

*May 24*

# AT THE WHEEL

*E*very person sits at the wheel of his own life with one foot on the accelerator, leaving the other for the brake. He needs to be awake. He needs to be alert. There are many wrecks along the way. Each travels at his own risk.

The journey demands that we follow the directions, observe the regulations, drive carefully, for it is our lives we are running. This is not a game or a dress rehearsal.

If we lose control for a moment, we crash. Though we have steered ourselves well ten-thousand times, there is never a time for intemperate driving. If we lose control, we crash.

*For a man to conquer himself
is the first and noblest of all victories.*
— Plato
428-348 B.C.

*And the driving is like the driving
of Jehu the son of Nimshi,
for he drives furiously.*
— II Kings 9:20

# BEAUTIFUL WITHIN

Appearances can be very deceiving. Green grass may cover the ground where dead men's bones lie. A healthy-looking tree may be ready to fall, a victim of its own rottenness within.

Sweet manners may be only skin deep; and if we should break the skin, we would be splattered with bitterness. A broad face does not necessarily mean a broad mind. A clean body cannot be equated with a clean life. A praying mouth does not always signify a praying heart.

It is not the cloth that makes the minister. Clothes change only the looks— not the person.

*I pray thee, 0 God,*
*that I may be beautiful within.*

— Socrates
469-499 B.C.

*For you are like whitewashed tombs*
*which indeed appear beautiful outwardly,*
*but inside are full of dead men's bones*
*and all uncleanness.*

— Matthew 23:27

# ONE MOMENT

Keep your patience! For if we lose it, we lose ourselves: your composure, confidence, assurance, will and success.

Patience is victorious: oftentimes outruns skill and outwits impulsiveness.

Patience is productive: in time the mulberry leaf becomes silk.

Patience is visionary: visualizes the ripened grain as the fruition of a series of successive steps of working and waiting— securing the land, breaking the soil and planting the seed. Nature is wise enough to wait and persistent enough to eventually have her way; and so can we if we will add patience to diligence.

Patience is the great possessor: the world belongs to the one who bides his time.

*One moment of patience may prevent disaster;*
*one moment of impatience may ruin a life.*
— Ancient Proverb

*For you have need of patience. . .*
— Hebrews 10:36

*May 27*

# SLAVES TO SUPERSTITION

Personal freedom is lost when we become cringing slaves to superstition. They, controlled by irrational thinking, become the bowing sacrificers to a supposed supernatural that is not supernatural.

The superstitious can't conquer the world, because they've been conquered by some stray cat, astrological readings or TV psychic. They are trying to solve life's problems through a hocus-pocus that pulls rabbits out of hats. That won't help them, but we can help ourselves. How? By being our own person, having our own mind, standing on our own feet, and pursuing our own dreams as we live our own fearless life.

*If not religious, man will be superstitious. If he worships not the true God, he will have his idols.*
— Theodore Parker

*Then Paul stood in the midst of Mars hill, and said, You men of Athens, I perceive that in all things you are too superstitious.*
— Acts 17:22

# A LITTLE CAKE

*I*t takes a little variety to season life. Sameness makes for lackluster. The same old routine gets deadly dull and exceedingly boring. Bread is the mainstay of life, but we need a little cake once in a while.

Variety gives life renewed enchantment. What about some stylish new clothes, different entertainment, varied topics for discussion, unvisited places to go, new scenes to see? Getting out of the rut is like crawling out of the grave. We can make this world a tomb, but God never intended it to be.

Nature with a thousand variations says to us, "The world is too exciting for you to ever be bored. Enjoy me."

*Variety is the mother of enjoyment.*
— Benjamin Disraeli
1804-1881

*For lo, the winter is past,*
*the rain is over and gone. The flowers appear on the earth;*
*the time of singing has come, and the voice of the turtledove*
*is heard in our land. The fig tree puts forth her green figs,*
*and the vines with the tender grapes give a good smell.*
— Song of Solomon 2:11-13

*May 29*

# FACES TO THE SUN

There are all kinds of "isms" in the world, and two that greatly affect us are of our own making: optimism or pessimism. Our victory or defeat lies mostly in the mind, in what we think we can or cannot do. Successful people are positive thinkers; failures think in negative terms.

There is no human power like that of confidence. The optimist says, "I'm sure there is a way," and rightly so; for the years have taught him that things have a way of working out, though sometimes slowly. And as they evolve, those who face the sun cannot see the shadows.

*God wants us to be victors, not victims; to grow, not grovel; to soar, not sink; to overcome, not to be overwhelmed.*

— William A. Ward
1812-1882

*If God be for us, who can be against us?*

— Romans 8:31

*May 30*

# NEARER HOME

With faith in immortality, it is easy to hold to the optimistic view that no day is wasted, though it is wrought with mistakes: It is used in the journey, and when twilight comes, we are one day nearer home.

Today is ours for us to use; and when it is over— good or bad— let us camp for the night; and at the dawn, pack up and move on, trusting, believing, never losing sight of our destination.

Our livelihood and comforts along the way are important, but not nearly as important as the faith that sustains us in our pilgrimage. This confidence makes life meaningful.

*To believe in heaven is not to run away from life;*
*it is to run toward it.*
— Joseph D. Blinco

*For man goes to his eternal home,*
*and the mourners go about the streets.*
— Ecclesiastes 12:5

*May 31*

# A SECOND SELF

reat your friends as friends should be treated: be sincere, considerate, courteous, truthful, loyal, sympathetic and helpful. If you are a friend, you will stay when others walk out; you will lend a hand when others fold theirs.

It takes time to make and hold friends; for relationships made fast seldom last. The "cannibal" who eats us up the first time he sees us will just as quickly move on to new friends.

Hold your friends close, but grant them freedom. Don't stifle them— let them breathe— for true friendship cannot survive when one is so smothered that there is no free breathing.

*A friend is, as it were, a second self.*
— Cicero
106-43 B.C.

*Do not forsake your own friend*
*or your father's friend.*
— Proverbs 27:10

*June 1*

## WE ARE THE ANSWER

The solution to all our problems has to come from within. It is more important to become and be than to get and possess. What we carry inside will take us farther than what carries us. We decide to allow Good to help us or not. We decide to follow one course or another. Our minds build barriers or demolish them.

Helen Keller definitely proved this. She came into the world with a twisted, tangled life, but she unravelled it. Born blind, deaf and mute, she was graduated with honors at Radcliffe. Her unconquerable spirit triumphed over all handicaps and lifted her to a place of glory.

*Give me, O Lord, a steadfast heart,*
*which no unworthy affection may drag downwards;*
*Give me an unconquered heart,*
*which no tribulation can wear out;*
*Give me an upright heart,*
*which no unworthy purpose may tempt aside.*
— Thomas Aquinas
1225-1274

*Our heart is not turned back.*
— Psalm 44:18

*June 2*

# WHEN MEDIOCRITY WINS

If anything turns up, ordinarily we will have to do the turning; and in most cases it requires more initiative than ability.

Mediocrity wins over superiority when it is used and superiority isn't.

A little talent and much application excel on most jobs. We don't have to have the most talent to win, but we do have to use it more. Short legs win over long legs provided we move them faster.

This leaves the road to success open to all— a little harder for some, but it is open.

*In this world and in every-day affairs,*
*you have got to run fast*
*merely to stay where you are;*
*and in order to get anywhere*
*you have got to run twice as fast as that.*
— Woodrow Wilson

*The king's business required haste.*
— I Samuel 21:8

*June 3*

# HINDERED BUT NOT DEFEATED

When the renowned Paganini's favorite violin was broken, he challenged the loss. Disappointed but not defeated, he got another one. "I will show them that the music is in me and not in any instrument," he avowed.

The way we meet the tests of life determines our fate. What makes a cynic is thwarted hopes mishandled. When one's plans have to be altered, he runs the risk of building up frustrations which harden into bitterness and cynicism. But there is no reverse that cannot be turned to some good. And there is no breakage of material things that can stop the melody of life. We will be hindered, but we don't have to be defeated.

*Men's best successes*
*come after their disappointments.*
— Henry Ward Beecher
1813-1887

*We are perplexed, but not in despair.*
— II Corinthians 4:8

# IT FEEDS ON ITSELF

We must never allow bitterness to sour our personality. No matter how hateful and heartless our circumstances may be, offset them with goodness.

Bitterness attracts bitterness and then multiplies by feeding on itself. It has a way of running to those who already have the most of it. But it shuns those with the greatest love and the highest degree of culture.

Trying to justify himself, the embittered person insists that he has cause for his condition. Maybe. Maybe not. Everybody has to drink from life's cup of bad breaks, but some have enough sweetness on the inside to dilute it— the bitter person didn't.

*The difficulties of life are intended to make us better,*
*not bitter.*
— Anonymous

*The heart knows its own bitterness.*
— Proverbs 14:10

*June 5*

# NEGATED INTO NOTHING

*N*egative thinking can negate us into nothing. Only the positive approach inspires the effort and releases the energy necessary to make a dynamic personality of achievement. Strong affirmatives give spirit, vitalize drive and attract friends.

Prophets of doom are not much in demand. The negative outlook is unpleasant, unhelpful and unproductive. Negativism sees bad where there is good. This repels would-be friends and defeats attainable success.

A dog will bark against what he thinks is bad when it could be the approach of a new-found friend. A negative bark and a cynical growl will never make us the pet of the neighborhood.

*With the right attitude, all the problems in the world will not make you a failure. With the wrong mental attitude, all the help in the world will not make you a success.*
— Warren Deaton

*The Lord is the strength of my life; of whom shall I be afraid?*
— Psalm 27:1

*June 6*

# UNION WITHOUT UNITY

*N*othing really unites people except agreement. The only genuine unity is found in like minds. It is hard for our bodies to walk together when our minds run in opposite directions. A group may seem to be united, which is nothing more than lip union with divided hearts.

Union without harmony of minds can be like a violin without a violinist— no discord, but no music either; or it may be like an off-key squeaky fiddle in an orchestra— sooner or later it must be tuned or they stop playing. Union without unison is unsatisfactory. Pleasant togetherness demands compatibility of views.

*Birds in their little nests agree;*
*And 'tis a shameful sight,*
*When children of one family*
*Fall out, and chide, and fight.*
— Isaac Watts
1674-1748

*Can two walk together, unless they*
*are agreed?*
— Amos 3:3

## June 7

# PLEASE PASS THE DECEIT

*N*othing makes us any sicker than swallowed deceit. Please don't pass us anymore. Though we have had our fill, we might take another helping. Why? For the same reason Eve did— it looks good; and, we admit, most of us are not as clever as we think we are, not as discerning as we should be.

Surely some pointers are in order: Be wary. Investigate. Talk it over. Think it over. Pray over it. Sleep on it. Chew on it, but don't swallow until you are completely satisfied that it is nutritious and digestible. For nothing is as hard to keep down as a plate of deceit.

*For of all the hard things to bear and grin,*
*The hardest is being taken in.*
— Phoebe Cary
1824-1871

*Did I not say,*
*Do not deceive me?*
— II Kings 4:28

*June 8*

## BE BRIEF

*L*ife is too fast for us not to be brief in our communications. Some reports which cover pages could be written on a note card. They remind me of a parrot that talked and talked and with all due respect to him, I had two criticisms: he was so repetitious and incoherent.

Brevity requires thinking, and this is no ordinary quality. The world's masterpieces of literature are brief: The Lord's Prayer of Example, sixty-six words. The Ten Commandments, reading time one minute. Lincoln's Gettysburg Address, about half a page.

Briefly concluded, that which takes too long to say, save it for eternity.

*Brief let me be.*
— William Shakespeare
1564-1616


*. . .for they think that they will be heard*
*for their many words.*
— Matthew 6:7

*June 9*

## BURY THE WORRIES

f we could bury our worries, we wouldn't have so many other funerals. Thus, let us consider some ways to put an end to one of the world's major killers— worry:

- Solve your problems rather than fret over them. Get expert advice, which can help you to temper anxiety into concern
- Look ahead, not back, for there is plenty of every thing up the line
- Dismiss from your mind every disturbance that cannot be righted
- While you realistically assess difficulty, have the habit of looking long at all of its possibilities for success
- And lastly, meet your problems only as they arise, for each day has enough of its own

*It ain't no use opening up our umbrella till it rains.*
— Alice Rice

*But take heed to yourselves,*
*lest your hearts be weighed down*
*with. . . cares of this life.*
— Luke 21:34

# LIKE A SORE THUMB

*R*eligion to some people is like a sore thumb that always gets in their way. Some wisely change their behavior; others give up their religion; and many more suffer the conflicting pulls. The latter two reactions remind us of the little girl who closed her evening prayer by saying, "Goodby, God; I'm going to town tomorrow."

But the very nature of religion is incompatible with total abandonment or half embrace. If we feel frustrated and disorganized, we can pull ourselves together by going one way. More commitment to God will resolve the divided heart and set both feet in one path.

*The Christian faith has not been tried and found wanting. It has been found difficult and largely left untried.*
— G.K. Chesterton
1874-1936

*If anyone desires to come after Me,*
*let him deny himself,*
*and take up his cross, and follow Me.*
— Matthew 16:24

# THE NAKED TRUTH NEEDS NO FIG LEAVES

It would be better to slap a person's face than to slip a lie in his ears— better for both.

Aside from the fact that telling a falsehood depraves the teller and deceives the told, it is just too bothersome. We can tell the truth and forget it, but a lie keeps making demands. The naked truth needs no fig leaves to hide it, while a lie is in constant need of more clothing. The task goes on and on.

A lie looks like a little convenience for the perpetrator, but it requires more cunning and a better memory than the liar has; so, he loses.

*No Man has a good enough memory
to make a successful liar.*
— Abraham Lincoln
1809-1865

*He who speaks lies will not escape.*
— Proverbs 19:5

*June 12*

# BY THE POUND

When I was a boy in the country, we had a mighty little rooster that was a mighty big crower. Finally when we got tired of it and took him to market, he was priced according to his weight rather than his noise and wing-flapping. Roosters are bought by the pound, not by the sound. Crowing doesn't bring anything in any market. No wonder, for it is all noise, not being, not doing.

As George Eliot said, "A donkey may bray a good while before he shakes the stars down." Bragging never accomplishes anything, not even in prayer. Lo, all our boasting today will be but nought tomorrow. How frantic! How vain! How futile!

*Do you wish people to think well of you?*
*Don't speak well of yourself.*
— Blaise Pascal
1623-1662

*For some time ago Theudas rose up,*
*claiming to be somebody.*
— Acts 5:36

## A LITTLE GRATITUDE

All of us like to be appreciated. When we send a gift to newlyweds or for a birthday present, all of us like to be thanked for our time, energy and money.

But while being thanked feels good, being thankful is even better for us. Developing an attitude of gratitude blesses us more than the ones we thank. A heart full of gratitude makes us more humble and less demanding, more happy and joyful and less concerned with having our needs met.

God has done a lot for us, at least we can be grateful.

*Thou hast given so much to me.*
*Give one thing more— a grateful heart:*
*Not thankful when it pleaseth me,*
*as if thy blessings had spare days.*
*But such a heart whose pulse may be Thy praise.*

—George Herbert
1831-1881

*Give thanks in all circumstances.*
— 1 Thessalonians 5:18

# NO USE TO COMPLAIN

It has been said that the wheel which squeaks the loudest gets the most grease. Yes, but only for a time; after awhile we discard it and buy a new wheel.

The habitual complainer soon loses his effectiveness.

Dogs growl, horses neigh and some people beef— frankly, I had rather listen to the dogs and horses.

Adjustment to what we cannot change is much more profitable than complaining about it. Changers and adapters— not complainers— lead our world. Grumbling about the weather will not change it, but we can change our clothes to fit it. And that's living!

*It is no use to grumble and complain;*
*It's just as cheap and easy to rejoice;*
*When God sorts out the weather and sends rain—*
*Why, rain's my choice.*

— James Whitcomb Riley

*And when the people complained,*
*it displeased the Lord.*

— Numbers 11:1

# NO MATTER WHAT YOU CALL HIM

A father may be designated by various appelations: if he is wealthy and prominent— "Father"; or if he tills the soil— "Pa"; or if he sits in shirt sleeves, with open collar, at ball games— "Pop"; or if he has a special talent for carrying bundles meekly— "Papa" with the accent on the first syllable; or if he is a reformer in our society— "Papa" with the accent on the last syllable; or if he is a genuine pal to his children— "Dad."

But no matter what you call him, in most cases he is the embodiment of all these characteristics, and to his children he is the greatest.

*Reverence and cherish your parents.*
— Thomas Jefferson
1743-1826

*Honor your father and mother,*
*which is the first commandment with promise.*
— Ephesians 6:2

*June 16*

# FATHER'S GREATEST JOB

*T*raining his children is the world's highest calling for any man. Gravest responsibilities. Greatest possibilities. For in teaching the better principles, father develops in his children the better character.

The best children, like the prettiest flowers and the sweetest music, are made by cultivation. The most fragrant flowers do not grow wild. The most beautiful music does not just happen. And the sweetest youth does not grow up pampered by parents and directed by self. It takes the dedicated mind and the determined hand of cultivation to bring out the best. And here the wise father performs his greatest job.

*One father is worth more*
*than a hundred schoolmasters.*
— George Herbert
1593-1633

*My son, hear the instruction*
*of your father.*
— Proverbs 1:8

## June 17

# FATHER DOES WHAT HE MUST

Father has a heart that loves, rejoices, bleeds and breaks like that of a woman, but most of the time he tries to hide it. His role, which calls for firmness, sternness and readiness for life's battles, may dim his softness; for he has to go out into the world of cold conflict and struggle to strive for those he loves.

Taking life's beatings without tears or complaints, grimly and steadily carrying on, fighting and toiling as he takes the reproaches and praises with the same smiling face and unchecked determination, rough and ready— father has a heart of gold, though the world often fails to see it.

*I like the man who faces what he must,*
*With steps triumphant and a heart of cheer;*
*Who fights the daily battle without fear.*
— Sarah Knowles Bolton

*For my father fought for you and risked his life,*
*and delivered you out of the hand of Midian.*
— Judges 9:17

*June 18*

# FATHER GETS SCHOOLED

Being a father is a schooling. It is an education to bear a child, provide for, train and educate him or her, and with anxiety of soul take the boy into your heart or hold that girl to your chest, watching with eyes that never sleep and with a foresight that never slumbers.

The father's verbal teaching and careful example, his living hope and the sharing of that expectation, his dauntless courage and the instilling of that determination in the heart of the youngster— these teach the child, but also the father. For there is nothing that educates the parent like the child.

*God has his small interpreters*
*The child must teach the man.*

— John Greenleaf Whittier
1807-1892

*You, therefore, who teach another,*
*do you not teach yourself?*
— Romans 2:21

*June 19*

# FATHER'S CARE RE-ENACTED

*N*ature's law of recompense is not faulty. The child must be protected. Years of care are necessary for the offspring to grow into manhood or womanhood. And during this time in which the world looks easy to youth, it is dealing the father strong opposition, serious setbacks and staggering blows.

Sons and daughters may not know this until the old man is dead and gone, but— they will learn. For by and by they will have children of their own, and the drama will be re-enacted. This time, however, the son who received has become the father and now divides his living with his own.

*There is never much trouble in any family where the children hope someday to resemble their parents.*
— William L. Phelps
1865-1943


*So he divided to them his livelihood.*
— Luke 15: 12

# FATHER THE HERO

We esteem father because of his heroism. His sweat and tears and blood shed for us testify to his heroic nature; for he who struggled for others when the easy way was to run is a hero, call him what you will. We were protected by his daily bravery.

The highest and noblest sacrifice is "that a man may lay down his life for another." Father did this— not in one supreme gift, but in giving of himself little by little, day by day. The daily conflicts of earning a living and heading a household brought out the slumbering qualities of the hero.

*Not at the battle front merit of in story,*
*Not in the blazing wreck, steering to glory;*
*Not while in martyr-pangs soul and flesh sever,*
*Died he— this Hero now; hero forever.*
— Dinah Maria Mulock Craik

*And we said to my lord,*
*"We have a father."*
— Genesis 44:20

*June 21*

# FATHER'S GRIEF

"*My* son, my son, would God I had died for thee" are the moving and emotional words which have been uttered by countless fathers through the ages.

Those words have been spoken in hospital rooms as the child slipped down through the valley of the shadow of death. That wailing cry has been heard in the silent cities of the dead as broken-hearted fathers tenderly and sobbingly, yet heroically, expressed their bleeding sorrow.

The qualities of his heart seem to be a thousand hearts— each an absolute necessity to fatherhood— and in this instance a heart of grief.

*That 'tis a common grief*
*Bringeth but slight relief;*
*Ours is the bitterest loss,*
*Ours is the heaviest cross;*
*And forever the cry will be,*
*"Would God I had died for thee,*
*O Absalom, my son!"*
— Henry Wadsworth Longfellow
1807-1882

*0 my son Absalom—*
*my son, my son Absalom—*
*if only I had died in your place!*
— II Samuel 18:33

*June 22*

# STRONGER THAN FEAR

*O*ur real strength is found in the strength of our convictions. We have to be sold before we can do a selling job. We have to believe in a thing before we are ready to stand for it.

Conviction refuses to court popularity; it defies opinion. And when conviction costs, no matter how much, the price is paid with the feeling that right is being done.

The most noble souls have always had convictions coupled with courage. Their convictions were stronger than their fears. Their belief was a compelling power that lifted their voices, raised their hands and moved their feet. They believed! And they stood!

*The only faith that wears well and holds its color in all
weather is that which is woven of conviction. . .*
— James Russell Lowell
1819-1891

*And so I will go to the king. . .
and if I perish, I perish.*
— Esther 4:16

# THE CLOCK REBUKES

*W*hile we complain of a lack of time, most of us have much more of it than we wisely use. Much of life is wasted in much ado about nothing.

We ought to learn from just looking at the clock's moving hands. What a forceful, though monotonous voice! Tick! Tick! Tick! They remind us that time is fleeting. They warn us not to waste our scarcest commodity— time. They exhort us to move on, appropriating the stuff that life is made of— time.

There are no precious earthly values except life and time, and one cannot be separated from the other.

*He who neglects the present moment*
*throws away all he has.*
— Johann von Schiller
1759-1805

*So teach us to number our days,*
*that we may gain a heart of wisdom.*
— Psalm 90:12

*June 24*

# THE MUD WE THROW

*S*ome people go around digging up dirt and slinging mud. But never— never— meet dirt with dirt. If we do, we will soon be spending most of our time wiping off mud and throwing it back.

Slinging mud at someone generally shows that he has considerable cleanness; otherwise why try to smear him? We seldom throw mud at people who are already covered in it.

There are worse things than being splattered with the hater's mud— one is to throw it back. Mudslinging soils the slinger more than the target. And knowing this, the public soon decides they prefer to deal with the clean-handed.

*Knowing, what all experience serves to show,*
*No mud can soil us but the mud we throw.*
— James Russell Lowell
1819-1891

*Repay no one evil for evil.*
— Romans 12:17

*June 25*

# NEVER A FAVORITE

A vulture will fly over a sweet-scented flower garden to seize a decaying carcass.

In like manner, the critic passes over many beautiful qualities in search of a fault. He has developed the habit. His captious eyes have warped his view. His satisfaction comes from assailment.

The faultfinder is never a favorite. He is not appreciated. No statue is ever erected to him. The world knows his judgment of others is only a reflection of his own state, that he has a knocking fist instead of a helping hand, and that he would serve a better cause if he would change his ways and be a model.

*He has the right to criticize*
*who has the heart to help.*
— Abraham Lincoln
1809-1865

*For in whatever you judge another,*
*you condemn yourself.*
— Romans 2:1

*June 26*

# HOLD THAT TEMPER

It's never good to strike while the head is hot. Steel loses its sharpness when it loses its temper, and so do we.

Anybody can lose his temper. Not hard at all. But to become angry at the right time, for the right purpose, in the right way, and in the right degree— now that is holding temper, and that is not easy.

But the bigger we are, we have more strength to hold what would be ungovernable urges within smaller and weaker people. The big person, loaded with coolness, rationality and tolerance, doesn't blow up quickly.

*Temper gets people into trouble.*
*Pride keeps them there.*
— Anonymous

*Let every man be swift to hear, slow to*
*speak, slow to wrath.*
— James 1:19

*June 27*

# WEIGHTIER THAN RUMORS

If we try to run down all innuendos and misrepresentations against us, we won't have time to get on a trail that leads to anywhere worthwhile.

The best answer to slander is to do our duty and say nothing. The evil that people hear about us proves nothing, but what they see and hear for themselves they know to be true.

The truth doesn't spread as fast as a lie, but it is weightier when it gets there. Eventually it will outweigh all rumors.

*Have patience awhile; slanderers are not long-lived. Truth is the child of time; ere long she shall appear to vindicate you.*

— Immanuel Kant
1724-1804

*Lead me, O Lord, in Your righteousness*
*because of my enemies;*
*make Your way straight before my face.*
*For there is no faithfulness in their mouth.*
— Psalm 5:8, 9

*June 28*

# BIGGER THAN TEMPTATION

We gain the strength of the temptation we withstand. Every person should make up his mind that he is bigger than the temptation which is trying to down him. If we do, we will get bigger as we stand. If we don't, we will get smaller as we fall.

We must learn what our temptations are, and we will know what we are. This self-discovery will give an insight to the weaknesses we need to work on the hardest. For it is better to recognize the fire than to try to cure burnt fingers.

We must pray for more power to resist! For the course of least resistance makes both rivers and humans crooked.

*God delights in our temptations and yet hates them. He delights in them when they drive us to prayer. He hates them when they drive us to despair.*

— Martin Luther
1483-1546

*My brethren, count it all joy when you fall into various trials, knowing that the testing of your faith produces patience.*

— James 1:2, 3

*June 29*

# WHEN CRITICIZED

We could not avoid criticism even if we were a corpse, said nothing, did nothing. It will come.

Though disapproval deflates, it can be helpful. If we stray, criticism can point us to the better way. If without erring we are criticized, even that can help us to avoid the error in the future. Furthermore, it can mellow us into being less critical of others.

It is our reaction to faultfinding— not what others say to us or about us— that blesses or hurts us. We can't help what some eyes may see in us, but we can help what lies within us.

*When men speak ill of thee,*
*live so no one may believe them.*
— Plato
428-348 B.C.

*Not returning evil for evil,*
*or reviling for reviling.*
— I Peter 3:9

# THEY DON'T LOOK UP
# IF WE LOOK DOWN

here are shortcomings everywhere. No question about that. The question is: What shall our attitude be toward the blemished?

Shall we be sympathetic or scornful? Shall we lift them up or tread them down? As we answer, remember: Our attitude toward them will determine their attitude toward us. No person will look up to us, if we look down on him. The holier-than-thou attitude doesn't work because it's too unrealistic to command respect.

As members of the human family, all err; and when one falls for the Tempter's bait, he needs the help of others to release him from the snare.

*We may dismiss compassion from our hearts,*
*but God will never.*
— William Cowper
1731-1800

*Brethren, if a man is overtaken in any trespass,*
*you who are spiritual, restore such a one in a spirit*
*of gentleness, considering yourself lest you also be tempted.*
— Galatians 6:1

*July 1*

# ACHIEVEMENT

Achievement! real achievement! consists of much:

- Self-command to turn on a day when it begins; self-discipline to turn it off when it ends
- Courage to accept a challenge, and the grit to persevere
- Determination to do what others think is impossible
- Admiration of the good wherever it is found
- Will to change what shouldn't be accepted; adjustment to accept what can't be changed
- Knowledge of self and honesty to face it
- Friendliness that causes a dog to wag his tail
- Gentleness that beckons a child to run after you
- And, lastly, finding joy in the simple pleasures of life, home and family.

*Do what you can
with what you have
where you are.*
— Theodore Roosevelt
1858-1919

*There is nothing better than to be happy and do good
while you live. That everyone may eat and drink and find
satisfaction in all his toil— this is the gift of God.*
— Ecclesiastes 3:12,13

*July 2*

# THE ROSES OF TODAY

Let today be mine, for I might not see tomorrow. May I take time to live before time takes me. The silver thread of life is too fragile to forfeit today for tomorrow. No one knows how much of this life is spent; but this we know: each day there is a little less.

As Longfellow said, "The young may die, but the old must." Thus the wisest program for living and dying is to make our plans as if we would trod the earth for a thousand years and so walk as if we would take the last step today.

*Live now, believe me,*
*wait not till tomorrow;*
*Gather the roses of life today.*
— Pierre de Ronsard
1524-1585

*There is but a step between me and death.*
— I Samuel 20:3

*July 3*

## A CHILD OF OPTIMISM

*R*emembering the past should make us a child of optimism. The passing years should have given us the hopeful disposition.

There have been many more victories than defeats. Most problems were not as hard as they seemed, and most difficulties worked out better than we expected. We never rolled and tumbled through a night that didn't end; nor witnessed a storm that didn't pass; nor traveled a rough road that didn't turn.

So we can take off our muddy glasses and see the world as it is: The earth is turning and the sun is shining— and we are alive!

*I am an optimist.*
*It does not seem too much use*
*being anything else.*
— Winston Churchill
1874-1965

*I have been young, and now am old;*
*yet I have not seen the righteous forsaken,*
*nor his descendants begging bread.*
— Psalm 37:25

*July 4*

# FREEDOM'S PRESERVATION

On this Fourth of July let us rededicate ourselves to the proposition that the people can be trusted to govern themselves. Let us resolve anew that this hallowed concept, bathed in the blood of heroic men and washed in the tears of courageous women, shall not perish by fault or default.

For democracy's success rests on us, the people: statehood rests on manhood, political self-government rests on personal self-government, national greatness rests on personal greatness, and liberty for all rests on restraint for each. Freedom's preservation truly lies in its true purpose: not the freedom to do wrong which hurts others, but the freedom to do right which helps all.

*Liberty exists in proportion to wholesome restraint.*
— Daniel Webster
1782-1852

*Righteousness exalts a nation,*
*but sin is a reproach to any people.*
— Proverbs 14:34

*July 5*

# I'D RATHER BE RIGHT

Henry Clay, one of America's most eloquent statesmen, had just proposed a political gesture to an associate.

"It will ruin your prospects for the Presidency," was the lightning response of his friend.

But just as quickly, Mr. Clay commented, "I had rather be right than President."

Switching the tags of right and wrong might have switched some votes in favor of Mr. Clay, but not the right of right and the wrong of wrong. It would have only disqualified him.

No matter what other qualifications we have, we can never be the right person for any job unless we plan to do right.

*The great man does not think beforehand of his words*
*that they may be sincere, nor of his actions*
*that they may be resolute—*
*he simply speaks and does what is right.*

— Mencius
372-289 B.C.

*Woe to those who call evil good, and good evil;*
*who put darkness for light, and light for darkness;*
*who put bitter for sweet, and sweet for bitter.*

— Isaiah 5:20

*July 6*

# ME INSTEAD OF PEDIGREE

*N*ot your ancestors, but you! Only you can make today yours! Good days are not found in the blood line, but in the line of duty. Who does something glorious for his descendants has no need for glorious ancestors.

It is better to have freedom than a line of kings in our ancestry; being free, we can rise to a place of recognition.

As we consider the family tree, don't forget that present fruits are more important than buried roots. There is more distinction in giving our posterity cause to brag about their ancestors than for us to brag about ours.

*It is indeed desirable to be well descended,*
*but the glory belongs to the ancestors.*
— Plutarch
46-120 A.D.

*And think not to say to yourselves,*
*We have Abraham as our father.*
— Matthew 3:9

# SOFT PILLOWS, SOFT HEARTS

*I*f we would have the unerring assurance that all is well, we must have a compass— conscience— that guides us as we study God's chart.

If we would have the aid of the one voice that means more than all other human voices, we must keep the approving words of the inner soul coming through loud and strong.

If we would have the most effective disciplinarian, we must find it in a sense of moral consciousness.

If we would have an inexhaustible source of refreshment for the day, we must awake each morning in harmony with yourself.

And if we would have the softest pillow for the night, we should sleep with a soft heart.

*A sleeping pill will never take the place*
*of a clear conscience.*
— Eddie Cantor
1892-1964

*For our rejoicing is this, the testimony*
*of our conscience. . .*
— II Corinthians 1:12

# THE CAUSES OF THINGS

Life must be lived under the unyielding law of cause and effect. Every effect has its cause. Comply with the rule and we shall be happy; violate it and we shall suffer.

It is about time we were learning the futility of trying to cure effects without remedying the causes.

The successful people in this world of sowing and reaping are smart enough to see the causes of things and strong enough to alter them. If we are successful, efficient and happy, it is no accident; it is the harvest of our own sowing.

> *Happy is he who has succeeded*
> *in learning the causes of things.*
> — Virgil
> 70-19 B.C.

> *. . .for whatever a man sows,*
> *that he will also reap.*
> — Galatians 6:7

# LIKE A TREE

The wind tests the trees. Only the strong ones withstand the force. The decayed and rotten ones crack and break under the strain.

The way a strong and heroic person withstands trials and afflictions reminds us of a tree planted by the rivers of water, which has deep unseen strength, for it is deep-rooted and well grounded. The ravaging storms sweep over it, the biting frosts creep round it, but it keeps on standing, producing fruit. So it is with some people. They possess a deep, unseen power that is adequate for every trouble. Their hidden strength sustains them in the storms that break others.

*The basic difference between physical and spiritual power is that men use physical power but spiritual power uses men.*

— Justin W. Nixon
1886-1958

*And he shall be like a tree*
*planted by the rivers of water.*

— Psalm 1:3

*July 10*

# NO EXCUSES

*Y*ou and I have troubles, and so does everybody else.

But they will be fewer and easier, if we meet them with the brave determination: Come when you will, trial and trouble, nature's appointed powers of discipline and refinement; I am ready for the challenge.

Trials have their compensations. Our world of difficulties was not designed to discourage and defeat, but to provide strength by conflict and melody by opposition. The oak grows strong by facing the opposing winds and the brook makes its music by running over the rocks. Nature accepts no difficulty. Neither does history.

*Difficulty is the excuse history never accepts.*
— Samuel Grafton

*You, who have shown me great and severe troubles,*
*shall revive me again, and bring me up again*
*from the depths of the earth.*
— Psalm 71:20

*July 11*

# REDUCING HARDSHIPS

Hardship comes to all, but it has a preference for the intemperate, the foolish, the fearful, the idler and the quitter. Oh, how hardship likes their company, so much that it stays with them.

But hardship doesn't like to associate long with the brave, the industrious, the believing and the wise; for they wrestle with it and overcome it. Trouble knocks them down occasionally, but they have a way of getting back up one step closer to better things. As victors, the blows knock them only toward grandeur.

*To overcome difficulties is to experience*
*the full delight of existence.*
— Arthur Schopenhauer
1788-1860

*Though I walk in the midst of trouble,*
*You will revive me.*
— Psalm 138:7

# THE SECRET OF ABSTINENCE

Abstinence comes easier with use. Its secret is found in refraining the present moment. Through use we develop power to resist or tendency to succumb. Triumph this moment, and the next is easier; fail, and the next is harder to win. For nature's rules cannot be mocked.

Overindulgence demands overpay, and will sooner or later collect. But abstinence is a benefactor with many professions—financier, physician, psychiatrist and minister—which gives money for the pocket, health for the body, clearness for the head, and peace for the heart.

Abstinence lets us remain in control!

*Refrain to-night,*
*And that shall lend a kind of easiness*
*To the next abstinence: The next more easy;*
*For use almost can change the stamp of nature.*
— William Shakespeare
1564-1616


*Abstain from every form of evil.*
— I Thessalonians 5:22

## SUCCESS IN FAILURE

For today to be mine, I need some goals even though I reach them not. If they should elude my striving and grasping, I shall still get more out of this day for trying.

There is such a thing as the paradox of achievement in nonfulfillment. If my working and praying do not bring me up to my aims, think how much lower I shall sink if I do not strive. So while I am trying, I am succeeding though I seem to fail. And come tomorrow I can try again. And that will be another success.

*Success is to be measured, not by wealth, power, or fame,*
*but by the ratio between what a man is*
*and what he might be.*
— H.G. Wells
1866-1946

*Uphold my steps in Your paths,*
*that my footsteps may not slip.*
— Psalm 17:5

*July 14*

# CHARACTER VERSUS REPUTATION

$\mathcal{R}$eputation is the name we have— not necessarily the character we are. It is what people think of us— not always what we know ourselves to be.

It glories in a world of vanities. And how vain a false reputation is! As Josh Billings stated, it can be obtained by giving publicly and stealing privately.

Reputation, of course, is valuable— a big asset— but character is better, character is priceless. A good reputation is only good business capital, but good character is goodness. Reputation can be obtained undeservedly or taken away without real cause, but character is left up entirely to us. . . only we can build it or destroy it.

*The reputation of a thousand years*
*may be determined by the conduct of one hour.*
— Japanese Proverb

*I know your deeds;*
*you have a reputation of being alive,*
*but you are dead.*
— Revelation 3:1

*July 15*

# HEAVEN TRIMS OUR LAMPS

*O*ur trust in God gives assurance for today and anticipation for tomorrow. It takes the fear and dread out of life. Even the clouds reflect a goodness and the night conveys a peace.

Trust says, "Take a step, another, and another," and on we go— planting crops, building houses, expanding business, entering school, switching jobs— looking to the dawn. We make plans. We strive to carry them out. We do the best we can for ourselves and trust God to bless our feeble efforts. Life is a benediction. The days are ours— and so are the nights.

*Heaven trims our lamps while we sleep.*
— Amos Bronson Alcott
1799-1888

*But as for me, I trust in You, O Lord;*
*I say, "You are my God."*
*My times are in Your hand.*
— Psalm 31:14, 15

## July 16

# ME IN THE DARK

The strength of an individual lies in his or her character. Just as no building can stand out of proportion to its foundation, no life can stand out of measurement with its moral values. A weak character cannot support a strong life.

Character is not something we develop in a crisis; it's what we exhibit in a crisis— but we had it all the time.

Character is the accumulation of many thoughts and many deeds— not one. It's what we have become! Me! Me in the dark! And what I really am is the only basis for anything worthwhile.

*A person never discloses his own character*
*so clearly as when he describes another's.*
— Johann Paul Richter
1763-1825

*If you faint in the day of adversity,*
*your strength is small.*
— Proverbs 24:10

# CAREFUL WITH CARES

*H*andle with care is my motto for handling life's cares; otherwise the cares will handle me and the day will be lost when it could be mine.

I need to be concerned with life, but must watch lest I become charged with anxiety, apprehension and worry.

Like roses, the concerns of life have their hidden thistles; and unless I deal with them discreetly, I shall be pricked without ever catching their fragrance.

Like riding on a plane, it is foolish to sit with my suitcase in my lap. It costs no more to lay the cares aside and relax.

*If your heart is troubled,*
*you are not living up to your belief.*
— Oswald Chambers
1874-1917

*And the cares of this world and the deceitfulness of riches*
*choke the word, and he becomes unfruitful.*
— Matthew 13:22

# TRUTH IS INDESTRUCTIBLE

*I*f we would find today good and tomorrow even better, we must give ourselves unreservedly to truth. Falsehood may take the day, but not tomorrow. Only the truth outlasts the days.

The world may try to run off and leave the truth, but tomorrow the unadorned realities will still be standing there and demanding that they be faced.

Truth is indestructible: club it, beat it, knife it, shoot it, strap it in the electric chair, but it refuses to die. It is immortal!

> *Truth, crushed to earth shall rise again;*
> *The eternal years of God are hers;*
> *But Error, wounded, writhes in pain,*
> *And dies among his worshippers.*
> — William Cullen Bryant
> 1794-1878

> *I have chosen the way of truth.*
> — Psalm 119:30

# PIETY PLUS

It is only natural to find a big dose of humanity in human beings. This means imperfection.

For one to pretend a super-piety puts his past under suspicion. The public is apt to come to the conclusion: Having committed all the sins there are, there is nothing left for this person but to exercise himself lamenting in saintly tones the mistakes of others. So now in proud disdain for sin he does refrain.

But there is no excellence in refusing to do that which one is tired of doing or no longer can do. What is virtue in a corpse is no virtue among the living.

*Youth should heed the older-witted*
*When they say, don't go too far—*
*Now their sins are all committed,*
*Lord, how virtuous they are!*
— Wilhelm Busch

*For all have sinned, and fall short*
*of the glory of God.*
— Romans 3:23

*July 20*

# A DRESSED UP LIE

*D*ressing up a lie just makes a bigger lie. The ornaments add to the wrong— make it more attractive but more hurtful, for now it is more deceptive.

Then why do people lie? Why do they clothe falsehood with more fabrications? They blindly think perversion will do more for them than truth. It is their crafty manner of acquisition. Their cunning form of equalization. Their supposed help in time of trouble.

But a lie can never be cleaned up by simply clothing it in white. A lie is a lie, dress it or undress it as you will.

*The essence of lying is in deception,*
*not in words; a lie may be told by silence,*
*by equivocation, by the accent on a syllable,*
*by a glance of the eye.*
— John Ruskin
1819-1900

*The truthful lip shall be established forever,*
*but a lying tongue is but for a moment.*
— Proverbs 12:19

*July 21*

# AGELESS TRUTHS

*I*t is always a new wonder how people can so easily reject that which is called old: old truths, old principles, old concepts, old slogans. Nothing is bad because it is old, and nothing is good because it is new.

Whatever has been so relevant as to outlast the ages deserves more than a hasty rejection. Look at the rubbish heaps of new ideas, painfully discarded and stacked higher and higher, before we remove the ancient landmarks. Those markers don't stand without purpose.

Though we call ageless truths old, actually they are younger than youth. That which defies time can never age.

*The public doesn't require any new ideas.*
*The public is best served by the good,*
*old-fashioned ideas it already has.*
— Henrik Ibsen

*Do not remove the ancient landmark.*
—Proverbs 23:10

*July 22*

# THINK AND THINK AGAIN

*T*hink! for it distinguishes us— raises us above the animal and makes him more like God.

Think! for it is the greatest human power— harness it as we will.

Think! for no brain is stronger than its weakest think— and thought by thought we forge the chain of success.

Think! for it is our chief vocation— no matter how we earn our bread.

Think! for it will shorten our job— whatever it is.

Think! for it is more essential to living than education— and more pertinent to fruition than grammar.

> *Less than 15 percent of people*
> *do any original thinking on any subject.*
> *The greatest torture in the world*
> *for most people is to think.*
> — Luther Burbank
> 1849-1926

> *O Lord, how great are thy works! and*
> *thy thoughts are very deep.*
> — Psalm 92:5

# A PRAYER FOR COURAGE

God, give me courage for this day. May I not turn coward before it's difficulties. May I prove equal to its duties. Come what will, let me cling to the philosophy that I am not beaten. Let me see myself not as a worm to crawl at other's feet, but as one who holds up his head and stands tall in the midst of all. May I never bow to failure, and when a setback comes, let me see it as only an experience for growth. Knowing that fear is a lack of faith and vision, may I believe, lift up my eyes, and walk unafraid.

*Do not ask the Lord for a life free from grief,*
*instead ask for courage that endures.*
— Anonymous

*Be of good courage, and let us be strong.*
— II Samuel 10:12

# THE GIFT OF ENCOURAGEMENT

*W*hat would happen if everyone we met today encouraged us and built us up and lifted our spirits? At first, we might be tempted to feel our pulse or call the newspaper to see if we had died and they had forgotten to tell us.

The person in the next office, the boy at the cleaners, the woman at the market could all be encouragers, but they are probably not. Few of us are; however, we could be, we could give the lavish gift of encouragement every day, free of charge. We could build up people— not with fake or phony flattery, but with real, meaningful expressions of encouragement and praise as they bear heavy burdens, solve difficult problems, or even as they perform routine tasks.

As we encourage others, we become encouraged.

*Encouragement is oxygen to the soul.*
— George M. Adams
1878-1962


*And let us consider one another*
*in order to stir up love and good works,*
*not forsaking the assembling of ourselves*
*together, as is the manner of some,*
*but exhorting one another, and so much the more*
*as you see the Day approaching.*
— Hebrews 10:24,25

# LET THE CHIPS FLY

In cutting wood, we can't worry too much about where the chips fall. No chips, no cutting, but no wood either. No offenses, no standing, but no character either.

A very famous woodcutter, Abraham Lincoln, once said, "Stand with anybody that stands right while he is right and part with him when he goes wrong."

We must ask: What is right? Not who is for it or against it. Observing where people stand on an issue only gauges popularity— a fickle thing— which comes and goes. But right is stable, and time and eternity are on the side of those who hew the line.

*He will hew the line of right,*
*let the chips fall where they may.*
— Roscoe Conklin
1829 -1888

*And Asa did what was right. . .*
— I Kings 15:11

# COMPLIMENTS TO THE SHEEP

When a wolf puts on sheep's clothing, he compliments the sheep. Being two-faced indirectly condemns the first and praises the second.

So there is evidence of good everywhere, even in hypocrisy. The hypocrite pays tribute to refinement, grace, good manners, and religion, though his heart is not in them. He knows their value or he would not put on their masks and parade as something he is not.

Hypocrites should encourage rather than discourage us. They prove the reality of the thing they mimic, that it is something good to be. We just need to recognize it.

*Hypocrisy is the homage that vice pays to virtue.*
— La Rochefoucauld
1613-1680

*Even so you also outwardly appear righteous to men, but inside you are full of hypocrisy and lawlessness.*
— Matthew 23:28

*July 27*

# THE ELOQUENCE OF SILENCE

*T*here are times when silence has the loudest voice. Occasions arise when the best way to say much is to say nothing. The eloquence of silence can be reprimanding, or consenting, or unanswerable, or persuasive, or peaceable. It can also be otherwise.

So, when do we speak and when do we refrain? The answers are an education in the School of Good Days: Say nothing when we have nothing to say, or when we have said enough, or when we don't know how to say it, or when it is the wrong time, or when it would hurt others, or when it would fall on deaf ears. This requires character.

*Silence is one of the hardest arguments to refute.*
— Josh Billings
1818 -1885

*And he answered him not one word,*
*so that the governor marveled greatly.*
— Matthew 27:14

# MORE THAN A LIVING

We owe it to ourselves to make more than a living— to make our living worthwhile. It is not enough to live and learn— we should learn and live. A little learning can add a lot to living. When we learn that life consists not in the abundance of the things we possess, we can do more living; we can live on less and enjoy it more.

The world owes us nothing— it was here first. We must earn our bread— and the right to enjoy it, which is accomplished through mental victories. We have life; what we do with it is our choice.

*Fear not that thy life shall come to an end, but rather fear that it shall never have a beginning.*

— John Henry Newman
1801-1890

*. . .for one's life does not consist in the abundance of the things he possesses.*

— Luke 12:15

# July 29

## VEIL OF GOLD

In this age of misplaced values, the package is prized beyond the contents, the clothes above the person, and the possessions more than the possessor.

The veil of gold owned by any family is expected to hide all its unseemliness— grandpa's backwoods origin, and grandpa's errant grandson and erratic granddaughter.

In the spirit of the times, if a person has a gold idol, there is no end to the long line of worshippers who will come to fall down before it. And he may think they are paying homage to him; but let him lose the money, and see what happens to the line.

*Living in the lap of luxury isn't bad,*
*except that you never know*
*when luxury is going to stand up.*
— Proverb

*Your gold and silver are corroded.*
— James 5:3

*July 30*

# TACTFUL WAYS

A little tact will often prevent resistance. It has the discernment and judgment to approach opposition at the least sensitive point. It is the seeing eye, the hearing ear, the easy step and the soft touch. Diplomacy knows how to do things, and thus increases the chances of success a hundredfold. Obstacles are not knocked down; they are climbed over skillfully. It turns adverse circumstances into advantages.

Tact wins, because it has winning ways. Here is the formula: Be rationally right; be affably aggressive; be politely plain; be effortlessly emphatic; be patiently positive; be gracefully gentle.

*Tact is the ability to remove the sting*
*from a dangerous stinger without getting stung.*
— James Bryce

*A man has joy by the answer of his mouth,*
*and a word spoken in due season, how good it is!*
— Proverbs 15:23

*July 31*

# DIFFICULTIES TRAIN US

*N*othing in life is so hard but what we can make it easier by the way we meet it. Difficulties are the trainers which develop character. By strengthening ourselves to overcome trials, we add to our might. All hindrances are tests. They try the reality of our resolutions and the genuineness of our purposes.

The hot sun tries the roots of the plants. The strong wind proves the tree's branches. The high hill tests the car's motor. So it is with us: when life is uphill, our character and faith are being tested— and developed.

*Many men owe the grandeur of their lives to their tremendous difficulties.*
— Charles H. Spurgeon
1834-1892

*For You, O God, have proved us;*
*You have refined us as silver is refined.*
— Psalm 66:10

*August 1*

## STEP BY STEP

Ambition can not help any of us unless we are practical. We must set our eyes on a star, but not forget to see it from the down-to-earth view. That will strike a balance between vision and workability.

It's never good to have our head so high in the air we can not see where we are stepping; nor so low we can not see to reach above ourselves. We can avoid a lot of falls by looking where we are going.

Adapting life to practicality, step by step, may not be the most visionary, but it is the most fruitful.

*A man gazing on the stars is proverbially*
*at the mercy of the puddles on the road.*
— Alexander Smith
1830-1867

*The wise man's eyes are in his head;*
*but the fool walks in darkness.*
— Ecclesiastes 2:14

# OUTLAST THE BLOWS

*S*uccess requires us to get up just one more time than we get knocked down.

That's what life is: getting knocked down and getting up; stay down and we miss half of life— the better half, the half that makes the whole worthwhile.

The blow may be a swinging door, a harsh word, lost job, a bad investment, a misplaced confidence, lapse in health, or a loved one's passing.

Whatever fells you, get up. If it only staggers you, gain your balance and renew the struggle. Outlast the blows— that's the secret of triumph.

It is hard! But it is harder to lose!

*We conquer— not in any brilliant fashion*
*— we conquer by continuing.*
— George Matheson

*Have I not commanded you?*
*Be strong and of a good courage;*
*do not be afraid, nor be dismayed.*
— Joshua 1:9

# August 3

# HOW TO STAY YOUNG

It can be our fortune to stay young. We can avoid old age. We really can! For age is only a quality of mind. We are young if we:

- Have turned loose of yesterday
- Enjoy today
- Anticipate tomorrow
- Look up when knocked down
- Feel there is much to learn
- Are ambitious
- Are enthusiastic
- Dream
- Have no wrinkles on the heart
- Feel young

But—

*If you have left your dreams behind,*
*If hope is cold,*
*If you no longer look ahead,*
*If your ambition's fires are dead,*
*Then you are old.*
— Anonymous

*How old are you?*
— Genesis 47:8

# BLUEPRINT FOR BETTER LIVING

*I*deals are the basis for character, the motive for achievement and the direction for destiny.

Having been defined as good, ideals arouse us to reach them. They are the power to fashion and shape human lives. They are the blueprint of higher living. They are the urgings of the better self.

Ideals will not let us settle for the low in life; they keep us reaching. They will not let us make a truce with evil; they keep us on the side of right.

What a lift it is to have such ideals that we can not get even close to reaching them without being elevated.

*Ideals are like stars; you will not succeed in touching
them with your hands. . . Choose them as your guides,
and following them you will reach your destiny.*
— Carl Schurz

*I have walked in my integrity.
I have also trusted in the Lord;
I shall not slip.*
— Psalm 26:1

*August 5*

## USING THEM ALL

We can sleep walk through life or we can give it all we have. Are we allowing our God-given talents to be dormant, or are we using them to the fullest? The intellect to search for deeper answers? The vision to see farther ahead? The heart to stick a little longer? The hands to tire less quickly? The feet to keep on climbing? The ears to hear sweeter melodies? The tongue to speak a kinder language— love? And a spirit to enjoy a superior fellowship— with God?

Learning to live is an art, and it takes a lifetime to finish the course.

*What small potatoes we all are,*
*compared with what we might be.*
— Charles Dudley Warner
1829-1900

*They go from strength to strength. . .*
— Psalm 84:7

*August 6*

# TOO SMART TO LIE

*I*t is neither right nor bright to lie. Its only hope of success is in keeping itself unknown. It can't stand investigation. And dealing in a trade that can't endure the light of day has a dark future.

A lie is a spectacle of hypocrisy deceitfully masquerading in the robes of integrity. Like a snake in the grass, it strikes. It is an infamous effort to cash in on falsehoods, zigzags and broken promises. It makes human relationships a travesty and a person's word a dagger in the mouth.

Goodness is too good to lie, and wisdom is too wise to do it.

> *He who tells a lie is forced to invent*
> *twenty more to maintain it.*
> — Alexander Pope
> 1688-1744

> *It is better to be poor than a liar.*
> — Proverbs 19:22

# PLAYING BLIND TO EVIL

*O*ne of our personal deficiencies is to play blind to evil. The course of least resistance is to close our eyes to wickedness. It is less disturbing to see no danger. But it is unthinkable that we would walk off a cliff, telling ourselves it is not there; or after we have plunged a thousand feet to exclaim, "Everything is all right so far."

To close our eyes and stop our ears changes nothing.

The first step in the reformation of a situation is the recognition of evil for what it is; the second is for it to become to us an insufferable wrong.

*Indifference to evil is more insidious than evil itself;*
*it is more universal, more contagious, more dangerous.*
— Abraham J. Heschel

*But evil men and imposters will grow worse and worse,*
*deceiving, and being deceived.*
— II Timothy 3:13

# SECOND FIDDLE

*N*ot everyone can be the best at his or her chosen activity. For some they want to be recognized at work, or at church, or at the golf course, or as a trend setter, etc. The list goes on and on.

And it is not a bad thing to want to excel and do our best. On the contrary, we should strive to excel. But we should also be humble enough to accept second place without feeling second class. There is a difference. Our self worth should not be tied to external measures that are so fickle and fleeting.

Let the other person get some of the spotlight. Better yet, we can even be happy for them.

*It takes more skill than I can tell,*
*To learn to play the second fiddle well.*
— Anonymous

*Be completely humble and gentle.*
— Ephesians 4:2

# August 9

## CONSCIENCE GIVES COURAGE

*No* one is braver than his conscience. If our conscience condemns, everything is frightening; a mouse looks like a giant; and the night is always long and spooky. On the other hand, if we have the approval of self, we are more apt to be unafraid and undaunted as we face the criticisms and condemnations of a misguided people.

The fearful cries of cowardice can be the self-made spooks of a hurting conscience; and conversely the fearless calls of true valor may be the amplified whisperings of an approving inner voice. So if you would keep your courage, keep your conscience.

*A person of honor would prefer to lose his honor*
*rather than lose his conscience.*
— Michel de Montaigne
1533-1592

*Then those who heard it,*
*being convicted by their conscience,*
*went out one by one.*
— John 8:9

## *August 10*

# BUSINESS BEFORE PLEASURE

An indispensable requisite of duty is that it be placed ahead of pleasure. The immaturity that causes one to abandon business for pleasure will wreck any hope of achievement.

Business success is very demanding— not accidental. It requires priority, thought, judgment, decision, daring, diligence, opportunity, work, drive, perseverance; but if we, in our pursuit of pleasure, relegate these necessities to secondary places, then we must take a back seat in the business world where there are fewer demands. It's sort of like sitting on the back pew at church— it requires less than the amen corner.

*Don't let yourself be diverted*
*from your duty until you have finished—*
*not even if a cannon goes off at your elbow.*
— Konrad Adenauer

*And food was set before him to eat, but he said,*
*"I will not eat until I have told about my errand."*
— Genesis 24:33

*August 11*

# MADE STRONGER BY NECESSITY

Like the little birds, we are not going to fly until we get shaken out of our nests; nor shall we develop the strongest wings until we try them against the wind.

The dove in the fable, perturbed because the wind ruffled its feathers, thoughtlessly wished for a firmament void of air that it might dart through empty space like lightning. Foolish bird! For without that air it could neither soar nor live.

Friends in struggle (and that's all of us), let us not foolishly wish away every opposition. It is better to meet and master our difficulties that we can be lifted higher and made stronger through conflict.

*The harder the conflict, the more glorious the triumph.*
— Thomas Paine
1737-1809

*For You have armed me*
*with strength for battle.*
— II Samuel 22:40

# THE BRAGGART

"*I* sure shook that bridge," said the mouse to the elephant after they had crossed it. So goes the brags of the self-praiser.

The only thing in his favor is he's not apt to have any rivals in praising himself. The world will let him have the floor on that subject. They think he must be a sham, or he wouldn't spend so much time talking himself up. The world appraises (not praises) him as an empty vessel, for he has those distinctive empty sounds.

If we want good things said about us, be praiseworthy and let others do it— not ourselves.

*A donkey may bray a good while*
*before he shakes the stars down.*
— George Eliot
1819-1880

*Let another man praise you, and not your own mouth;*
*a stranger, and not your own lips.*
— Proverbs 27:2

*August 13*

# THE BOTTOMLESS CUP

Self-righteousness is an ugly, bottomless cup; though the self-lover pours and pours, he is never able to fill it. Pouring himself into himself adds nothing. No wonder! For nothing plus nothing equals nothing.

He wants to look big, but goes at it backwards. He should have more interest in being than in seeming, and then he would humbly pour himself out of himself into the service of God and humanity. Now that adds something: real righteousness, wholeness of self. And that's what fills the cup.

God will fill our cups, but only when they are empty of pharisaical impurities.

*The Lord gives his blessing*
*when he finds the vessel empty.*
—— Thomas À Kempis
1380-1471

*But we are all like an unclean thing,*
*and all our righteousnesses are like filthy rags;*
*we all fade as a leaf; and our iniquities,*
*like the wind, have taken us away.*
— Isaiah 64:6

*August 14*

# PURSUIT OF PURPOSE

As we clarify and focus our aims, we raise or lower our standing. We are not likely to reach what we do not aim at. In the pursuit of aimlessness we are sure to find it—nothing!

In contrast, it is through purposes that we capture fortune, for we go out to find it.

By aiming we marshal our forces: employ our talents, use our time, harness our strength and direct our quests. With all this going for us, we are sure to go places we otherwise would not. And though we do not reach our goals, we find achievement in purpose.

*Everyone should have a goal*
*for which he is willing to exchange*
*a piece of his life.*
— Carlyle Boehme

*And, behold, I purpose to build a house*
*for the name of the Lord my God.*
— I Kings 5:5

*August 15*

# THE NECESSITY OF ETHICS

*S*trive mightily, but maintain the highest ethics in debating our causes. For we can win the argument and lose the person. Winning at any price is too big a price; for then we have lost. Winning is definitely not winning unless it is ethical.

Cutting our opponent's throat doesn't put a halo on our head. Remember— cut-throats are not much in demand, for no one wishes to be abused. Unquestionably, we haven't triumphed unless we are in demand when we get through.

So, press your cause, prod it, propel it, push it, pull it, but don't forget to be friends to those who stand in the way.

*And do as adversaries do in law,*
*Strive mightily, but eat and drink as friends.*
— William Shakespeare
1564-1616

*Debate your case with your neighbor himself.*
— Proverbs 25:9

# POOR COMMUNICATION

The person had nothing to say and he cursed; maybe this is why— he had nothing to say. Another one had something to say and he swore; maybe this is why— he knew not how to say it. And another had something to say and he could have said it, but didn't; he swore, and maybe this is why— habit.

In all three cases, it was poor communication. Each wasted his breath in an unprofitable and abominable custom. Showing irreverence toward our Creator does not lend force to language, nor to personality; and it certainly does not manifest courtesy to others who have to listen.

*To swear is neither brave, polite, nor wise.*
*You would not swear upon the bed of death:*
*Reflect! Your Maker yet may stop your breath.*
— William Cowper
1731-1800

*You shall not take the name of the Lord*
*your God in vain.*
— Exodus 20:7

# WHAT IS PRAYER?

What is prayer? The flight of men and women to the bosom of God. Infirmity leaning on Infinity. Misery wooing peace. The gathering together of inner resources. The unity of body, mind and spirit, which gives powerless people powerful strength. The key that unlocks the morning, and the bar that bolts the night.

It is a sure position which keeps us from standing in our own way. It is a natural impulse when the well runs dry, when the storm hits, and when the death angel hovers. It is the one place every child of God can go when all other places are closed.

*Prayer is the simplest form of speech*
*That infant lips can try;*
*Prayer the sublimest strains that reach*
*The Majesty on high.*

— James Montgomery
1771-1854

*To You, O Lord, I lift up my soul.*
— Psalm 25:1

*August 18*

# MORE PATIENCE

For more power, develop more patience. It can make a Job out of every one of us.

Patience hopes in sickness, purposes in prosperity, and holds on in poverty. It is unrestrained by intolerance, unmoved by reproach, unshaken by slander, and unblended by persecution. It produces faithfulness in church, harmony in families, success in business, and magnanimity in society.

Patience controls the anger, bridles the tongue, and restrains the hand. It endures hardships, rides out the storm, picks up the pieces and builds anew. It sees a new day and awaits the dawn. It does too much not to be working for me.

And when we pray for patience, maybe we should pray for it right now!

*Never think that God's delays are God's denials. Hold on;*
*hold fast; hold out. Patience is genius.*

—Comte de Buffon
1707-1788

*The end of a thing is better than its beginning,*
*and the patient in spirit is better than*
*the proud in spirit.*

— Ecclesiastes 7:8

# THE GOLDEN YEARS

*N*ature has a way of compensating us for the loss of youth; as the years come in which we must use our bodies less, experience has prepared us to use our minds more. As much as our physical prowess is treasured, it is not comparable to intellectual competence.

The riper years can be the golden years: a time in which we can find blessedness in our own company, an accumulation of experiences which guard against phantoms, a maturity which has become fed up with youth's sucker bait, an unfoldment of more hindsight which gives deeper insight and longer foresight. Yes! They can be the best years!

> *Strike when thou wilt, the hour of rest,*
> *But let my last days be my best.*
> — John Greenleaf Whittier
> 1807-1892

> *They shall still bear fruit in old age.*
> — Psalm 92:14

# PRIDE'S INDIGESTION

*S*ome people have indigestion because they have trouble swallowing their pride. And if it were not so inflated, it would not be so hard to swallow. It's too big.

Don't get me wrong: It's all right to hold up our heads— we should— but do so without turning up your noses. Now it's the turned-up-nose crowd that is so proud of so little. They crave halos when they are not holy, chief seats when they are not leaders, honor when they are not honorable, and recognition while they hope that what they are will not be recognized.

They have fed on the wrong stuff— and are overstuffed.

*Proud people breed sad sorrows for themselves.*
— Emily Brontë
1818-1848

*A man's pride will bring him low,*
*but the humble in spirit will retain honor.*
— Proverbs 29:23

*August 21*

# USE THE KEY

If you would have, look to self. I have seen the principle work in the lives of many. I knew a banker who went bankrupt, as many did, in the Great Depression. Undefeated, he began on foot to sell used clothing from house to house. Later he opened a used clothing and furniture store. Next he went into the oil business and became prosperous again.

The world awards its prizes to people of self-reliance. And so does God! Let self-dependence be a part of our religion; for, after all, God helps those who want to be helped and are willing to be partners with Him. No locked door will open for us unless we use the key we have been given.

*God gives every bird its food,*
*but he does not throw it into the nest.*
— Josiah G. Holland
1819-1881

*She considers a field; and buys it;*
*from her profits she plants a vineyard.*
— Proverbs 31:16

## TO HIT A STAR

It was the colorful P. T. Barnum, the circus king, who said, "If I shoot at the sun I may hit a star." We don't always reach our aims, but how much higher we rise because we try. Attainment is no accident. Having no aim means no success. No aspiration grows leaden feet!

Every person is capable of raising himself. There are two requirements: first, look up and second, walk up. The higher we aim, in keeping with reality, the more transcendent we become; but aiming no higher than the alarm clock would help some people.

*One half of knowing what you want*
*is knowing what you must give up*
*before you get it.*
— Sidney Howard

*Therefore we His servants*
*will arise and build.*
— Nehemiah 2:20

# SEEKING GOOD ADVICE

It is easy to get advice. All we have to do is catch a cold. The trouble is: most of it is not worth very much. Comes free, but is still greatly overpriced. Now we shouldn't let this close our ears to wise counsel. Just be sure it is good!

It takes wisdom merely to seek wise advice, to know where to look and how to appraise it. We shouldn't listen to the failures! Look elsewhere. Seek guidance from knowledgeable men and women of experience and common sense. Then there is the problem of following it, which takes more than genius.

*Advice is like snow; the softer it falls, the longer it dwells
upon and the deeper it sinks into the ground.*
— Samuel Taylor Coleridge
1772 -1834

*Every purpose is established by counsel;
by wise counsel wage war.*
— Proverbs 20:18

# HOW ARE OUR GRADES?

*A*ffliction is the school that lasts a lifetime; no one ever graduates until he steps all the way across the stage into the next world. Every person is a student; the courses vary with individuals, but each has his own load.

Painful and trying, no school does more for us than the School of Affliction, if we are apt learners. In every hurt, there can be a lesson that develops character, increases sympathy, adds to patience, fortifies for disappointment, firms will power, lifts the eyes to see the more valuable values, and multiplies wisdom by prodding one to think deeper.

We are all students together. How are our grades?

> *God will not look us over for medals,*
> *degrees, or diplomas, but for scars.*
> — Elbert Hubbard
> 1856-1915

> *For our light affliction, which is but for a moment,*
> *is working for us a far more exceeding*
> *and eternal weight of glory.*
> — II Corinthians 4:17

# BUT DON'T PULL DOWN THE HEDGE

In fulfilling our duty toward our neighbor, we should keep a pleasing manner and a smiling face. Strive to make ourselves a source of pleasure to him. Be sincere. Be humble. Be encouraging. Be consoling. Follow after the things which make for peace. Conceal his faults and mistakes, remembering that we have ours. Express appreciation for the kindness he renders us. Compliment him, but don't flatter him. And when we err, as all humans do, never take it out on him— apologize. And last of all, as Benjamin Franklin said, ". . .don't pull down your hedge."

*The love of our our neighbor is the only door*
*out of the dungeon of self.*
— George Macdonald
1824-1905

*Everyone helped his neighbor, and said to his brother,*
*"Be of good courage."*
— Isaiah 41:6

# EXTOLLING THE PAST

It is not wise to minimize the present by maximizing the past. The past was good, but perhaps not as good as some would have us think. Its presently perceived excellency is not so much in blue-ribbon accomplishments as in an inclination to over appreciate it now because it was under appreciated then.

Furthermore, as our future shrinks, there is a tendency to swell the past. This accounts for much of the praise heaped on yesteryears. While they were wonderful, most of the merit is in our minds. And if we made the past so sweet, we can do the same today.

*That sign of old age, extolling the past at*
*the expense of the present.*
— Sydney Smith
1771-1845

*Do not say, "Why were the former days better than these?"*
*For you do not inquire wisely concerning this.*
— Ecclesiastes 7:10

*August 27*

# A CEMETERY FOR RUMORS

If all the rumors were true, surely none of us would be worth shooting; but all of us would be rich. There are rumors about people's sins, and there are rumors about "gold in the hills"— investments. But usually the gold is not there, and in most cases neither is the sin. If we can be fooled by believing in fool's gold, then are we not bigger fools for believing every rumor about some person's frailty?

One of the fine things about a cemetery is it spreads no rumors. Why not have a cemetery just for rumors? And if we start by burying rumors about others, maybe they will bury the ones about us.

*There's only one thing as difficult
as unscrambling an egg,
and that's unspreading a rumor.*
— Anonymous


*Disaster will come upon disaster,
and rumor will be upon rumor.*
— Ezekiel 7:26

# WHAT WILL THEY FIND?

*E*ach generation has the right to use the world, but not abuse it. The who-cares philosophy, which gets what you can, anyway you can, as long as you can, leaves a wasted world in its wake.

If our hands are thieves which snatch the wealth of ages; if our feet plod and trample nature's provisions; if we are a people whose sensitivity is seared to polluted streams, poisoned air, huge debts and dog-eat-dog morals, we are more than exploiters— we are culprits whose sins shall affect the unborn.

So let us ask: When we vacate this old world and the new tenants move in, what will they find?

*It pays. . . to try and do things,
to accomplish things in this life,
and not merely to have a soft and pleasant time.*
— Theodore Roosevelt

*One generation passes away, and another generation comes;
but the earth abides for ever.*
— Ecclesiastes 1:4

*August 29*

# A PRAYER FOR CLEAN HANDS

*O* Lord, help me to keep my hands clean. May I have hands that never steal; hands that never take a bribe; hands that know no greed; hands that move when there is work to be done; hands that mind their own business; hands unsoiled with broken trusts; hands that never knife a friend in disloyalty; hands that never hold back any one; hands that never cheer when others fall; hands that are never raised in angry blows; hands unstained with the blood of the innocent; hands that are fit for the other person to shake.

*God takes notice of clean hands, not full hands.*
— Latin Proverb

*Yet the righteous will hold to his way, and he who has clean hands will be stronger and stronger.*
— Job 17:9

# PROPAGANDA CAN MAKE
# EVEN SATAN LOOK GOOD

*P*ropaganda often is the prop for error. Indoctrination can change people's thinking, but not facts. You can whitewash wrong and brainwash people; but when you get through, neither has been laundered. You can't change the color of sin by calling it something else.

Sugaring over the devil does not sweeten him nor us; to try it, leaves bitterness in the mouth. For guile is always bitter, even though it is sugar-coated. And to rid it, one must replace the evil with the sweet truth. This demands investigation, discernment and the necessary sacrifice to make the exchange.

*With devotion's visage*
*And pious action we do sugar o'er*
*The devil himself.*
— William Shakespeare
1564 -1616

*. . .will you not cease perverting*
*the straight ways of the Lord?*
— Acts 13:10

# MORE PRECIOUS THAN RUBIES

*W*isdom is priceless. This quality is unquestionably high on the list of personal values. The Bible commends it; the philosophers praise it; the poets extol it; and the wise seek it.

Sir W. Temple said, "A man's wisdom is his best friend; folly, his worst enemy."

Defined, wisdom is the use of knowledge and experience in meeting successfully the circumstances of life. It puts ready hinges on the door of success and a soft glove on the fist of fate. Some call it common sense. Whatever it is, the wise get more of it; but fools, never.

*We can be knowledgeable with other men's knowledge,*
*but we cannot be wise with other men's wisdom.*
— Michael de Montaigne
1533-1592

*Wisdom. . . is more precious than rubies;*
*and all the things you may desire cannot compare with her.*
*Length of days is in her right hand,*
*and in her left hand riches and honor.*
*Her ways are ways of pleasantness,*
*and all her paths are peace.*
— Proverbs 3:13-17

# THE GOOD TEACHER

*S*ay all that humanity has ever said about a good teacher, and you won't say half enough. The great teacher gives more than ideas— ideals, more than facts— inspiration, more than cold answers— warm provocations to think, and more than a knowledge of the past— a challenge for the future.

He or she deals with the noblest work of God and the only real thing of value— human hearts. Everything else is secondary.

The excellent teacher makes the ideal teaching situation, no matter how many teaching aids are lacking.

*Give me a log hut, with only a simple bench,*
*Mark Hopkins on one end and I on the other,*
*and you may have all the buildings, apparatus*
*and libraries without him.*
— James Abram Garfield
1831-1881

*And he began to teach them many things.*
— Mark 6:34

# A COLLARLESS SOCIETY

*W*ithin our sophisticated society, certain forms of work and labor are looked down on. Oh, we don't have to list them here, we all know the kinds we are talking about.

But before we get too smug, we need to remember this: society could not exist without all members of the family of labor. The person who labors with his head would be under a tree if it were not for the man who works with his hands. And what kind of TV would you be watching if you had to make it yourself?

Blue collar— white collar— no collar, we need each other.

*No race can prosper till it learns*
*that there is as much dignity in tilling a field*
*as in writing a poem.*
— Booker T. Washington

*Command those who are rich in this present world*
*not to be arrogant...*
— 1 Timothy 6:17

# WORK WITH A VISION

*D*oing all we can for ourselves is based on thought and toil, encouraged by faith and supported by perseverance. God wills us well in life; but if God's will is done, we must perform our work.

The state of comfort and ease is not as pleasant as some think. It is wrought with disappointments: muscles weaken, eyes drop and hearts lose their zest. No interest! No challenge! No stimulation!

When we get a little too comfortable, maybe we need another mountain to climb, at least a hill, for down-hill living lowers us.

*A task without a vision is drudgery;*
*a vision without a task is a dream;*
*a task with a vision is victory.*

— Anonymous

*Fulfill your works, your daily tasks ...*
— Exodus 5:13

# WHEN HARVEST COMES

A lazy person and a fruitless tree go together—the tree makes the shade, the indolent sits in it. Neither produces.

Hard work plants the seed and reaps the fruits. Laziness harvests nothing, nothing but woes.

Industry clears the mind, strengthens the body, guards the soul and fills the wallet. It encourages honesty and peacefulness, for there is less temptation to steal and cause trouble. It gives a satisfaction and contentment that idleness can never know. And if I had to choose one or the other, I had rather have industry without genius than genius without industry.

*Labor disgraces no man;*
*unfortunately you occasionally find men*
*who disgrace labor.*
— Ulysses S. Grant

*Slothfulness casts one into a deep sleep;*
*and an idle person will suffer hunger.*
— Proverbs 19:15

# THE SUCCESS FAMILY

Whole-heartedness and Success
Diligence and Victory
Indolence and Failure
Unsteadfastness and Defeat

*H*ere we have four sets of Siamese twins, and the whole world knows they belong together as we have linked them.

But indolence and success, unsteadfastness and victory, are not even fourth cousins; so there is no way to relate them. For only like kind are like kin.

The Success Family is very distinctive. It has no lazy children.

*I never knew an early rising, hard-working, prudent man who complained of hard luck.*
— Joseph Addison

*The plans of the diligent lead surely to plenty.*
— Proverbs 21:5

# THE RIGHT OF WAGES

*L*abor was appointed at the creation, but so was its remuneration. "In the sweat of thy face shalt thou eat bread." Labor and sustenance go together. The right to enjoy the fruits of his work is one of mankind's earliest rights, stretching all the way back to the dawn of time. It is a God-given due.

If we deny a person his just wages, we deny him the freedom to live. We take his life, if we take that which sustains life. Toil should not go unrewarded! Even the working animal is entitled to eat.

*Labor, if it were not necessary for our existence, would be indispensable for the happiness of man.*
— Samuel Johnson

*You shall not muzzle an ox while it treads out the grain.*
— Deuteronomy 25:4

# A THOUSAND TIMES HARDER

It is hard for us to be what we ought to be, but it is much harder not to be.

It is not easy to earn a living, but it is a lot easier than starving or begging or stealing.

The price of morality is high, but the price of immorality is even higher.

It is tiresome to bear our burdens, but to refuse to bear them is not restful.

There are bitter circumstances which test our politeness, but rudeness sweetens nothing, only adds bitter to bitters.

It is hard to do anything meritorious, but it is a thousand times harder to fail.

*We conquer— not in any brilliant fashion*
*— we conquer by continuing.*
— George Matheson

*You have shown Your people hard things.*
— Psalm 60:3

# AN OUNCE OF LOYALTY

*L*oyalty gives unmixed support. It is true in word, faithful in deed, devoid of hypocrisy, free from betrayal; and when Judases sell out, it can't be bought.

Loyalty is so appreciated that the world treasures one ounce of it more than a pound of cleverness.

Therefore, whatever relationships we have that demand loyalty, we must be true to them. If we hire out to a person, work for him. If he supplies our bread and butter, we should supply devotion and dedication. As long as we work at a place, work for it. Give an undivided service or none. If we can't be loyal, leave.

*If you are ashamed to stand by your colors, perhaps you had better seek another flag.*

— Anonymous

*And you know that with all my might*
*I have served your father.*

— Genesis 31:6

# DIFFICULTIES DEVELOP US

*D*on't fret because of difficulties. They show what we are made of.

When obstacles are piled high and we climb over them, we have ascended higher than we would have without them. They are nature's way of developing strength. Just sitting in an easy chair and eating off a silver platter is no way to develop our best.

It takes strenuous effort to climb a mountain, but half the joy of looking from the peak is due to the difficult climb. And traveling a pathway of thorns teaches doggedness, caution, sympathy, and consequently the goal is more appreciated.

*The Lord gets his best soldiers*
*out of the highlands of affliction.*

— Charles H. Spurgeon

*That in a great trial of affliction,*
*the abundance of their joy and their deep poverty*
*abounded in the riches of their liberality.*

— II Corinthians 8:2

*September 10*

# OF BOOKS AND FRIENDS

how me the company a person keeps and the books he reads, and I shall tell you what kind of a person he is. For where there is attraction, there is likeness. Some literature appeals. And some people are his kind.

Each person seeks to please himself. If a book doesn't satisfy, then he's not going to read it. Neither will he maintain associations that are unenjoyable. He gravitates toward the people of which he is a part; and he goes out from certain others, because he is not of them. Like minds move toward togetherness; unlike ones move their feet— in opposite directions.

*Show me his friends and I the man shall know;*
*This wiser turn a larger wisdom lends:*
*Show me the books he loves and I shall know*
*The man far better than through mortal friends.*
— Silas Weir Mitchell

*They went out from us, but they were not of us;*
*for if they had been of us,*
*they would have continued with us.*
— I John 2:19

# PARROTS OR PEOPLE?

*M*en and women are so constituted that when they are struck with a thought, it ought not to be an accident. Our distinction is our ability to think for ourselves.

When brains don't think— even though educated— the person is caged within the confines of what another gives him, good or bad. Little cages are for thinkless parrots, but the wide universe is for thinking men and women. The heavens and the earth welcome those who think; if we don't, we must remain in our cages and parrot cute little phrases for those who feed us.

*Thought takes man out of servitude, into freedom.*
— Henry Wadsworth Longfellow
1807-1882

*If anything is excellent or praiseworthy,*
*think on these things.*
—Philippians 4:8

# THE GOOD LIFE

For life to be the fullest, sweetest and most rewarding:

- Do more than move; improve
- Do more than get; give
- Do more than regret; repent
- Do more than look; see
- Do more than sympathize; help
- Do more than attend church; worship
- Do more than have children; rear them
- Do more than build a house; make a home
- Do more than breathe; live
- Do more than live; love


*We live in deeds, not years; in thoughts, not breaths,*
*In feelings, not in figures on a dial.*
*We should count time by heart-throbs.*
*He most lives*
*Who thinks most, feels the noblest, acts the best.*
— Philip James Bailey


*We spend our years as a tale that is told.*
— Psalm 90:9

# CHANGE THE CAUSE

*E*very consequence has a reason. Hence, if we would improve our lot, we must work on the causes. This is better than whining over unsatisfactory results. Shaping causes is our prerogative; and as we do, we change ourselves and the world.

This is what life is all about— causes and effects. We plant a crop and reap a harvest, dig a well and have water, throw up a dam and make a lake, slant our minds and so become ourselves.

This principle distinguishes the corrector from the complainer, the gainer from the grumbler, the haves from the have-nots.

> *Don't curse the darkness—*
> *light a candle.*
> — Chinese Proverb

> *Is there not a cause?*
> — I Samuel 17:29

# THE COIN OF COURTESY

*C*ourtesy pays. To the receiver it produces happiness. To the exhibitor it adds both personality and fortune.

It opens hearts which, in turn, opens purses. A wealthy merchant stated that he owed his fortune to Joseph, of the Old Testament, from whom he had gleaned his business policy: "The customer is right, though he is wrong." He found it more profitable in the end to exhibit a special courtesy to the purchaser than to contend for his own rights. Courtesy is truly a coin that is valued in any nation.

*We must be as courteous to a man as we are
to a picture, which we are willing to give
the advantage of a good light.*
— Ralph Waldo Emerson
1803-1882

*And he comforted them and spoke kindly to them.*
— Genesis 50:21

*September 15*

# SUCCESS DEMANDS HONESTY

The highway of success is not wide enough for crooked dealings. It shouts to the traveler, "If you would travel me, leave behind deceit, dishonesty and skullduggery." It is a road for only the upright. Though it may appear that the dishonest can traverse it, sooner or later they hit the bumps and land in the ditch.

The honest journeyer has the advantage of being able to travel day or night, but the crook has a feeling of false security in only night driving.

The road to success looks narrow, but it is wide enough to handle the traffic.

*Friends, if we be honest with ourselves,*
*we shall be honest with each other.*
— George Macdonald
1824-1905

*The integrity of the upright will guide them.*
— Proverbs 11:3

# THE NEW SPIRITUALITY

The new wave of an increased desire for "spirituality" must give God quite a laugh. To see His fortunes rise and fall with the stockmarket must be very interesting to the Maker of Men and Spirit of Spirituality.

If we were God, we might not be so ready to accept all the "new converts" who formerly thought we were some old-fashioned symbol of a bygone day. Now that religion is back in vogue, everybody wants to be "spiritual."

Isn't it wonderful that our God, the real God, is bigger than we are, more accepting than we are, more forgiving than we are. No probation, no waiting period. He is ready to become everything to us. All we have to do is to accept his call.

*Spiritually, we never grow old.*
*The characteristic of the spiritual life is its unaging youth,*
*exactly the opposite of the natural life.*
— Oswald Chambers
1874-1917

*I will pour out my Spirit on all people.*
— Joel 2:28

# ATTITUDE—NOT BIRTHDAYS

The only true gauge of life is action— not pounds and inches. And the only true measurement of age is attitude— not birthdays.

This is why some people become old at thirty, while others remain young at eighty. Let's not confuse age with anniversaries. Though we have seen fourscore years, we are just ripening youth if we:

- Love life
- Enjoy living
- Are hopeful
- Seek new thoughts for stimulation
- Find new ways to do old things
- Raise new ladders to climb
- Enter new fields to gather

Threescore or fourscore— who's keeping score?

*Few people know how to be old.*
— Francis de La Rochefoucauld
1613-1680

*I am this day fourscore and five years old.*
*As yet I am as strong this day as*
*I was in the day that Moses sent me.*
— Joshua 14:10, 11

# BETRAYED FROM WITHIN

*S*elf-loyalty! An ingredient of every worthwhile person, organization or business.

We can survive the betrayal of supposed friends, but not self. In tragic life, the disloyalty that destroys is within. There the plot thickens. There the villain resides. The Judases without are not half as deadly as the Judas within. Others can let us down and we can still come out on top, but not if we let ourselves down. It is hard to recover from self-inflicted wounds.

Be true to self and you can look friend and foe in the eye; betray yourself and you'll never be able to look anybody in the eye.

*We are betrayed by what is false within.*
— George Meredith

*Create in me a clean heart, O God,*
*and renew a steadfast spirit within me.*
— Psalm 51:10

# NO GARLANDS FOR IMITATORS

*W*e are worth more being ourselves than trying to be somebody else. It saves us from having to act— no theatrical performances. Neither do we have to suffer the mockery life heaps on the pretender. Furthermore, our singleness of personality— not multiple selves— brings an internal peace never known by the imitator.

Being ourselves is more impressive; no make-believer is believed very long. It gives more energy; acting is hard work. It affords habitual and spontaneous reactions, because there is no delay in trying to read another's lines. We can be independent; for trying to be another is like being the tail on another dog— he wags us.

*Posterity weaves no garlands for imitators.*
— Johann Christoph Friedrich von Schiller
1759-1805

*Why do you pretend to be another person?*
— I Kings 14:6

# ONE VOLUME LIBRARY

*A* knowledge of the Bible is essential to scholarship in many fields. The libraries of the world are to a large extent commentaries and elaborations on the principles laid down in the Bible. It is truly a one volume library.

The person who knows the Bible is a scholar and if he follows it, a saint. "Of making many books, there is no end," but none takes the place of the Book. It is as inexhaustible as dipping up the ocean with a spoon. It challenges the best minds, and though they read it a thousand times, something new is gleaned from every reading.

*I thoroughly believe in university education*
*for both men and women, but I believe a knowledge*
*of the Bible without a college course is more*
*valuable than a college course without the Bible.*

— William Lyon Phelps
(Called the most beloved professor
of America—of Yale University.)

*Your word is a lamp to my feet, and a*
*light to my path.*
— Psalm 119:105

# THE LAST WORD

aving the last say does not say you are first. Any person with the biggest muscle and the least brain can have the last say. Greatness is not in the last word, but in the wisest word. And the wisest word is often no word— silence. We are seldom hurt by what we don't say.

When peace is threatened, it is better to draw on our self-control and say nothing than to draw on our vocabulary and say something that adds nothing. A good talker knows when. Who keeps his tongue, keeps peace— and friends.

*The last word is the most dangerous of infernal machines,*
*and the husband and wife should no more fight to get it*
*than they would struggle for the possession*
*of a lighted bombshell.*
— Douglas Jerrold
1803-1857

*A fool's lips enter into contention,*
*and his mouth calls for blows.*
— Proverbs 18:6

*September 22*

# THERE HAD TO BE A CRISIS

We never recognize those worthy of fame until the test comes. The greatness is there all the time, but it takes the testing to discover it. There had to be a historic cause before there could rise a historic George Washington.

Think of the many greats whose names could be handed down to the ages, but who, because of a lack of testing, shall sleep in barely known graves that shall soon lose their little distinction. Untried, they walk along with the mediocre, hardly distinguishable. It's the crisis which distinguishes people, allowing one to surpass another.

Look around. We are surrounded by men and women fitted for greatness when the time comes.

*Greatness lies, not in being strong,*
*but in the right use of strength.*
— Henry Ward Beecher
1813-1887

*...And have made you a great name,*
*like the name of the great men who are on the earth.*
— II Samuel 7:9

*September 23*

# A COOL FRIENDSHIP

Perhaps there is nothing that cools friendships quicker than ingratitude. It is a member of a wicked family: pride, selfishness, unhappiness, baseness. The proud are not thankful— too hard for them to bow; neither are the selfish— feel they have everything coming; nor are the malcontented— nothing thrills them; nor are the base— their character is too weak to be thankful.

About all the ingrate is good at is biting the hand that hands him favors— a hand-biter.

Thank you! how inadequately it expresses our feelings. But until we come up with a better word, we should learn to say it over and over again.


*Who does not thank for little will not thank for much.*
— Ancient Proverb


*For men will be lovers of themselves, lovers of money, boasters, proud, blasphemers, disobedient to parents, unthankful, unholy.*
— II Timothy 3:2

# GENIUSES IN BLUE JEANS

Clothes do not make the man or woman of character. You can hang a coat on anything. A soiled life can wear cologne or perfume. A scoundrel can dress in a silken suit. A fake can sit behind the wheel of a late model car, if he makes the payments.

Like wise, men and women of quiet dignity and integrity may be often overlooked because they do not have the flash and fizz of the in-crowd. They stand in the shadows— geniuses in blue jeans, Einsteins in a t-shirt.

Why not today try looking beyond the externals— beyond the clothes, cars and corporate logos. Try looking at what God sees. Try looking at the heart.

*Do not conceive that fine clothes make fine men, anymore than fine feathers make fine birds.*
— George Washington
1732-1799

*The Lord does not look at the things man looks at. Man looks at the outward appearance, but the Lord looks at the heart.*
— 1 Samuel 16:7

# PEACEFUL PURSUITS

The enjoyment of peaceful days is not an accident; it is an achievement. The Pleasant Life is always conditional and one of the conditions is the pursuit of peace.

Peace and pleasantness just go together in a cause and effect relationship in which each promotes the other; and the result is the enhancement of health. So if we want health and happiness, we will seek peace and pursue it.

Peace is found where it is lost— in our attitudes and in our hearts. Thus we can find it again when, as partners with the God of Peace, we cultivate the things that make for peace.

*All men desire peace,*
*but very few desire those things that make for peace.*
— Thomas À Kempis
1380-1471

*Whoever would love life and see good days must keep his tongue from evil. He must turn from evil and do good; he must seek peace and pursue it.*
— 1 Peter 3:10, 11

*September 26*

# FORTUNE IN MISFORTUNE

Misfortune has its fringe benefits, even though we seldom recognize them at the time. Much of our soul-searching, resolutions, alterations, trust, sympathy and even prosperity have come to us through what appeared to be great disasters.

The story has been told of a poor miller whose mill and home were washed away by a flood. Standing on the site, feeling helpless and hopeless, he saw something shining in the muddy river bank. It was gold. That which impoverished him made him rich. And so it may be with us. Our adversity may become our gold.

*Fire is the test of gold; adversity, of strong men.*
— Lucius Annaeus Seneca
8 B.C.-A.D. 65

*When He has tested me,*
*I shall come forth as gold.*
— Job 23:10

# TAUGHT BY THE YEARS

The years should teach us that to "rush in where angels dare to tread" is the surest way to get knocked down and dragged out; that fairness requires hearing both sides; that we had to grow before we were prepared to accept some opportunities we wanted too early; that if we cut out the fear of things that never happen, we will reduce our troubles ninety percent; that common sense and love in our hearts will solve most problems; that Satan's lies are deliciously deceitful; and that God can be trusted to be good and faithful, kind and gracious.

*The years teach much which the days never know.*
— Ralph Waldo Emerson
1803-1882

*Days should speak, and multitude of years should teach wisdom.*
— Job 32:7

# ANGELS CAN DO NO MORE

*D*o your best. Not even the elements can do better. For a raindrop can give only so much moisture; a star only so much light; and a human being only so much productivity. Nature functions to its full capacity, and so should we.

If it is good to live up to our potential, then it is not good to drop below it. Nature has decreed that we live up to our talents and opportunities or lose them.

After we have done our best, there is only one other thing we can do— trust God for the rest. Angels can do no more.

> *. . .learn to do thy part*
> *And leave the rest to Heaven.*
> — John Henry Newman
> 1801-1890

> *Zaccheus. . . sought to see who Jesus was,*
> *but could not because of the crowd,*
> *for he was of short stature. So he ran ahead*
> *and climbed up into a sycamore tree to see Him,*
> *for He was going to pass that way.*
> — Luke 19:2-4

# ONLY THE FEARLESS ARE FREE

*W*e must conquer fear or be a slave. No slave chains or iron bars are as restricting as fear. It is ridiculous for us to talk about "the land of the free and the brave" while we wear the ball and chain of fear.

No person is free who is afraid to try lest he fail; or who fears to break with tradition; or who is scared to stand for right when only a few are willing; or who is frightened to speak the truth when the masses hold to error; or who is too cowardly to be his own master.

*They are slaves who fear to speak*
*For the fallen and the weak;*
*They are slaves who will not choose*
*Hatred, scoffing, and abuse,*
*Rather than in silence shrink*
*From the truth they needs must think;*
*They are slaves who dare not be*
*In the right with two or three.*

— James Russell Lowell
1819-1891

*I was afraid. . . and I hid myself.*
— Genesis 3:10

# MAKING LIFE COUNT

Life is too short and precious to waste. It is wrought with too many possibilities for accomplishment and happiness to fling it away. We must not squander ourselves on the frustrating dissipations of cynicism, hate, envy, retaliation, faultfinding, pessimism, gossip, idleness, doubt, debauchery.

So far, so good. No one would disagree. To make life count is the goal of every normal being. But count for what? To truly count, a life must get outside itself— into the lives of others; get beyond itself— into the hands of God.

*I will not just live my life.*
*I will not just spend my life.*
*I will invest my life.*
— Helen Keller
1880-1968

*Above all else, guard your heart,*
*for it is the wellspring of life.*
— Proverbs 4:23

# RADIANT HOPE

othing brightens the day more than anticipation. It quickens our heart and sets our soul aflame. It gives courage "to bear those ills we have." Anticipation guards every day against dullness and despair. It bridges our adversities.

We are creatures of hope; our world is a place of hope; and the person without it is a misfit. There are no hopeless situations; only hopeless people who make situations appear hopeless. Hope never says, "Let's quit." Though the night is dark, hope knows that every day has a morning. Hope hands us an easier today, for it anticipates a better tomorrow.

*O hope! Dazzling, radiant hope! What a change thou bringest to the hopeless; brightening the darkened paths, and cheering the lonely way.*

— Aimee Semple McPherson

*And you would be secure,*
*because there is hope.*
— Job 11:18

*October 2*

# KNOW WHEN TO BEND

$\mathscr{E}$very hour brings its own troubles. Hence, how do we handle the little worries, disappointments and tensions of everyday living?

In the first place, we must be realistic enough to know that they will come. A willing acceptance of them makes for calmness and rationalism as we face them.

Secondly, we can soften each blow by bending with it. By stooping with sweet condescension we lessen the impact. Bending when we can is preferable to breaking, and submitting where there is no violation of principle is better than being crushed. The merit is in solving the problem— not in rebelling at it.

Thirdly, maybe God is using the bending process to shape us into a stronger tree or a more graceful vessel. God can do that you know.

*Better to bend than break.*
— Scottish Proverb

*Listen to counsel and receive instruction,*
*that you may be wise in your latter days.*
— Proverbs 19:20

# BAG OF TRICKS

*I*nvestigate! Watch the deceivers and defrauders, fleecers and flimflammers, hoaxers and hypocrites. We should look before we leap. That soft landing prepared by the humbugs may be jerked out from under us.

The scoundrels are professors of virtue, but not possessors of it. They are artists in deception, actors who make quackery sound good. They count on our gullibility, our disinclination to investigate.

They carry a bag of tricks: They play on honesty when they are dishonest; they appeal to truth when they are liars; they say they love us when they love themselves; and they quote Scripture even when they don't believe it.

*The devil can cite Scripture for his purpose.*
— William Shakespeare
1564-1616

*And he said to Him, "If you are the Son of God, throw Yourself down. For it is written: 'He shall give His angels charge concerning you.' "*
— Matthew 4:6

*October 4*

# FORGET ABOUT IT

Pass it by! The slur, the slight, the catty remark we suffer from others. A refusal to forget it would keep us in war always. Our circle of friends would diminish; our blood pressure would go up; and our efficiency would go down. After all, most of us need just about as much tolerance from others as they need from us.

We should never be insulted by any moral and well-bred person, for he would not intentionally do it. Neither should we be affronted by any others, for they are not worthy to hurt us.

*A moral, sensible, and well-bred man*
*Will not affront me, and no other can.*
— William Cowper
1731-1800

*The discretion of a man makes him slow to anger,*
*and it is to his glory to overlook a transgression.*
— Proverbs 19:11

*October 5*

# MATTER OF MASTERY

There is no way to excel without exerting a greater power than the opposing forces wield. That is what triumph is— overcoming rather than being overcome. Success or failure is simply a matter of mastery— we conquer or get conquered.

Our world is one of struggles. We become educated by outsmarting ignorance; courteous by prevailing over rudeness; industrious by winning over slothfulness; superior by outdoing inferiority; and good by overcoming evil.

In all these tests we first struggle within ourselves where we first win or lose. Take heart— for we shall overcome.

*Not in the clamor of the crowded street,*
*Not in the shouts and plaudits of the throne,*
*But in ourselves are triumph and defeat.*
— Henry Wadsworth Longfellow
1807-1882

*A man is a slave*
*to whatever has mastered him.*
— II Peter 2:19

*October 6*

# CONQUERED FAULTS

*U*nless our virtues have come through self-determination and rigorous development, we cannot fancy ourselves as victors. There is no test of goodness in being polite toward the affable, patient toward those we fear or whose favor we court, or charitable toward those whom we love.

But there is merit— real merit— in conquering our faults. Take one— just one: gossip, slothfulness, sulkiness, uncharitableness, revenge, pride, envy, swearing or impulsiveness, and attack it bravely. It will take weeks— not to completely eradicate it— just to prevent it from dominating us. And it will be much easier if we read the Instruction Manual from our Divine Manufacturer. With that one subdued, we can then tackle another. It takes effort, but it gives satisfaction.

> *We rise by the things that are under feet;*
> *By what we have mastered of good and gain,*
> *By the pride deposed and the passion slain,*
> *And the vanquished ills that we hourly meet.*
> — Josiah Gilbert Holland
> 1819— 1881

*. . .put off the old man. . . put on the new man. . .*
— Colossians 3:9, 10

# BLESSED BY BOOKS

*B*ooks! What treasures! Old books make us heirs of the distant past. New books pull us into closer contact with our contemporaries. Old or new, books convert the reader's mind into a throne where knowledge reigns. And where knowledge rules, poverty is overcome, sorrow is healed, misery is cured, and oppression is lifted from bent and broken backs.

There is some hope for a person who reads good books, especially the kind that make us think. Get in the habit of carrying a volume with you. Have a nightcap book that climaxes the day with enrichment before you sleep.

*How many a man has dated a new era in his life
from the reading of a book.*
— Henry David Thoreau
1817-1862

*Bring the cloak that I left with Carpus at Troas
when you come— and the books,
especially the parchments.*
— II Timothy 4:13

# THE LITTLE THINGS

*C*herish the little things. They are often the most precious. Little words are the sweetest to the ear: God, church, Bible, faith, hope, love, mother, home, child.

Most of life revolves around the littles— little words and little deeds— but they are so necessary that they are enormous. A little cup of cold water, given a thirsty traveler, is big in the sight of heaven. Little songs enrapture the fullest. Little hearts arouse to the widest-eyed excitement. Simple joys last the longest.

A life full of little things becomes a majestic thing, especially when we ask God to bless it. He takes the little, and with Heavenly arithmetic, multiplies it infinitely.

*God does not want us to do extraordinary things; he wants us to do the ordinary things extraordinarily well.*
— Charles Gore

*Taking the five loaves and the two fish...*
*he gave thanks. And the number of men*
*who had eaten was five thousand.*
— Mark 6:41-44

# EASIER MADE THAN PAID

"*E*asy Payments" are not always easy. Slavish liabilities will cost us today, for we will have to pay it in worry and sweat and blood to others.

If we can't refrain from buying the things we can't afford, our obligations will pile up like mountains; and then life will be an uphill pull for us— too much to lug and too high to climb.

There are better ways of living than defaulting on debts that continually cause creditors to beat paths to our doors.

There was a time when delinquent debtors were stoned; today they are "billed" to death.

*Debt and Misery live on the same road.*
— Russian Proverb

*Do not be one of those who shakes hands in a pledge,*
*one of those who is surety for debts;*
*if you have nothing with which to pay,*
*why should he take away your bed from under you?*
— Proverbs 22:26, 27

# SILENT WORDS

*O*ur deeds say more than our words. In fact, they are the loudest, yet silent, words of all. What we do is what we are. What we say may be only what we want others to think we are. Mankind becomes the story of his own deeds; they make the man, and they tell what kind of man they have made. You might mistake a man's creed, but not his deed.

A busy tongue with still hands is inappropriate. Remember— nobody appreciates the sound of the clock unless there is movement of the hands.

*A few thousand words*
*will not leave so deep an impression as one deed.*
— Henrik Ibsen

*A certain man had two sons; and he came to the first,*
*and said, Son, go work today in my vineyard.*
*He answered and said, I will not; but afterward he repented,*
*and went. And he came to the second, and said likewise.*
*And he answered and said, I go, sir; and went not.*
*Whether of them twain did the will of his father?*
— Matthew 21:28-31

# October 11

## BLESSED TO BLESS

*I*t is a principle older than ancient Rome, Greece or even Egypt: when we are blessed, it is not for us alone. We are blessed so that we may in turn bless others.

In a remarkable call, God spoke to Abraham and blessed him. But it was not just for him. He was to go forth in faith and "all peoples on earth will be blessed through you."

Abraham is dead and gone, but the principle remains. It is true for us and will be true for our children. We must begin to live this way, unselfishly sharing and giving. We should teach our children to do the same.

*As the purse is emptied, the heart is filled.*
— Victor Hugo
1802-1885

*I will make you into a great nation*
*and I will bless you;*
*I will make your name great*
*and you will be a blessing.*
— Genesis 12:2

*October 12*

# A NEW WORLD

We too can discover a new world.
We can if we are willing to:

- Desire a world better than the one we now occupy
- Have faith that it exists, that it is not fantasy. It is as real as one wishes to make it. Believe we can find it, for we can
- Launch our ship. Lift the anchor. Set the sails, and no matter which way the wind blows, we shall be carried on our way
- Persevere. There are no happy lands over yonder for the fainthearted. We must have the spirit of Columbus who sailed on and on

*They sailed. They sailed. Then spoke the mate:*
*"This mad sea shows its teeth to-night. He curls his lip, he lies in wait, With lifted teeth, as if to bite!*
*Brave Admiral, say but one good word. What shall we do when hope is gone?" The words leapt as a leaping sword,*
*"Sail on! sail on! sail on! and on!"*

— Joaquin Miller

*He raises the poor from the dust and lifts the beggar from the ash heap, to set them among princes and make them inherit the throne of glory. For the pillars of the earth are the Lord's, and He has set the world upon them.*

— I Samuel 2:8

# HUMILITY, NOT HUMILIATION

*T*he truly great person never feels any honest task is too low for him.

When James Madison completed his eight years as President, he retired to his Virginia plantation and filled the office of justice of the peace. No wonder he had climbed up, for he knew how to climb down. He didn't have to appear to be great, for he was; and no office could make him less. His meekness was not weakness. His humility was not humiliation.

The size of the job is not half as honorable as the size of the person who fills it.

*I believe the first test of a truly great man*
*is his humility.*
— John Ruskin
1819-1900

*By humility and the fear of the Lord*
*are riches and honor and life.*
— Proverbs 22:4

# October 14

## ONE BLOOD

*A*fter all is said, there is but one race— mankind and to it every person belongs. All have the same lineage, a common ancestry. Thus we are all the master race with dominion over every other creature.

And in the gain or loss of one person the whole race is lifted or lowered. If there is hope for humanity, we must find it in and for all. Being of the same ancestry, blood should be stronger than prejudice; it is, and in time shall prevail.

Maybe we can begin showing a little more compassion and tolerance toward some of our distant cousins. Maybe there is not as much distance between us as we thought.

*We be of one blood, ye and I.*
— Rudyard Kipling

*And He has made from one blood every nation*
*of men to dwell on all the face of the earth.*
— Acts 17:26

*October 15*

# LED BY OUR THOUGHTS

*I*n our fast-moving world, take time to step aside and think. Later we can pass up the ones who didn't. Unless there is straight thinking, there can be no straight traveling. To avoid leaving zigzag and back tracks on the sands of time, we must use our heads for more than a decorative accessory. For as we think, we travel. Thinking can figure out the shortcuts. This is why some people are always ahead— they outthink the rest of the people.

However thinking is not always quick. While some are clamoring for action, we may need to put the matter aside, deliberate, pray. Even with a thoughtful delay, we can come out on top.

*The more you think, the more time you have.*
— Henry Ford

*I thought about my ways, and turned my feet*
*to Your testimonies.*
— Psalm 119:59

# PASS THE PRAISE

*P*ass on the praise! For all are mortal enough to love it. Its helpfulness, however, is found in its being deserved. This is what separates it from flattery. And everyone has something worthy of praise. Look for it. Tell them about it.

An appreciative word may create a new resolve. Praising something you like in a person, any person, invigorates him. If a person is good at a thing, tell him he is; if he gets better, tell him again; if he becomes best, tell him again. It will help him— and you— to tell him.

*We blossom under praise like flowers in the sun; we open,*
*we reach, we grow.*
— Gerhard Frost

*Her children rise up and call her blessed;*
*her husband also, and he praises her.*
— Proverbs 31:28

*October 17*

# CHURCH CLOTHES

When I was young, I had three kinds of clothes to wear: play clothes, school clothes and church clothes. Now you can probably guess the quality and price range of each set.

While church clothes today have gotten a lot more casual, like some other elements of church, a few people still put on something special for church, like a cloak of respectability or a robe of piety.

But church was never intended to be a fashion show. It is a time and place to honor God, draw near to our fellow believers, and to build up one another.

*Encouragement is oxygen to the soul.*
— George M. Adams

*Let us not give up meeting together,*
*as some are in the habit of doing,*
*but let us encourage one another...*
— Hebrews 10:25

*October 18*

# NO WILL, NO WAY

Hold the reins! Don't be a runaway.

An old stage-driver, after thirty years of experience, commented that he had never hurt a passenger nor a horse, simply because he always kept a firm grip on the reins. "The whole secret is in not letting the horses get the start," he said.

This is good philosophy for controlling self: Hold the reins; hold ourselves back from bad habits. We never become a runaway in a thing we never start. No one is stronger than his will. Unless we have will power, we will have no power. For where there is no will, there is no way.

*No horse gets anywhere until it is harnessed.*
*No steam or gas ever drives anything until it is confined.*
*No Niagara is ever turned into light and power*
*until it is tunneled. No life ever grows great until it is*
*focused, dedicated, disciplined.*

— Napoleon Bonaparte
1769-1821

*But I discipline my body*
*and bring it into subjection.*
— I Corinthians 9:27

*October 19*

# THINK BEFORE SPEAKING

*I*t is easier to say what we think than to think about what we say. There is wisdom in holding back the full utterance of our minds for the more opportune time. Knowing what to say and when to say it will put us among the great and the peaceful and the happy!

When we have a thing to say, say it, but not until we know how and when. Be sure it does good. An excellent rule to follow is to say only what we would be willing to have on our lips if they should never speak again.

> *He that would live in peace and ease must not*
> *speak all he knows nor judge all he sees.*
> — Benjamin Franklin
> 1706-1790

> *A fool vents all his feelings,*
> *but a wise man holds them back.*
> — Proverbs 29:11

*October 20*

# GENEALOGICAL FRUIT

It is desirable to have renowned blood, but the praise belongs to our forefathers, not us. The only glory I can claim is what I earn. I am just a limb on a genealogical tree; and if it bears fruit today, it has to bear it through me.

The plain fact is— every family line has the good and the bad, the king and the slave. Who my great-great-grandfather was is not half as important as what his great-great-grandson will be. Thus, it is fitting that I give less thought to my ancestors and more attention to this offspring of theirs.

*Who serves his country well*
*has no need of ancestors.*
— Voltaire
1694-1778

*Solomon did evil in the sight of the Lord,*
*and did not fully follow the Lord,*
*as did his father David.*
— I Kings 11:6

## COURTESY OPENS HEARTS

*H*earts are apt to open for us, if we use the priceless key of courtesy. It fits almost every locked heart.

Like responds to like. Use a courteous approach and we will get a courteous reception— with few exceptions. However, we should be courteous because of who we are, not for what we can get.

We can't storm into hearts— they are opened from within. And they open better if the hinges are lubricated with the oil of graciousness. It prevents friction. It is a smoothness that finds easygoingness everywhere.

Politeness is so necessary to better relations that it should be a part of every person's religion. In fact it is religion! For it is an expression of the Golden Rule.

*Courtesy pleases him who gives*
*and him who receives, and like mercy,*
*it is twice blessed.*
— Anonymous

*The words of a wise man's mouth are gracious.*
— Ecclesiastes 10:12

# THE BEAUTY THAT WINS

*G*ood looks are at a premium everywhere. Appearance is an asset to any creature, but not the ultimate in values. A person with good looks and fine physique has an advantage, but not enough to win without a winsome personality, charming manners, sterling character and a sharp mind.

Comeliness commends, but never wins— in the long run; for in the home stretch it is the inward beauty that years can't fade, that comes in ahead. There are born beauties, but no born winners. Handsomeness nor beauty never makes the person, but it may make him or her more marketable.

And if our own personal beauty is a little more "under the skin," maybe we should let it be a little more visible.

*Beauty, unaccompanied by virtue,*
*is as a flower without perfume.*
— French Proverb

*But the Lord said to Samuel,*
*"Do not look at his appearance*
*or at the height of his stature,*
*because I have refused him."*
— I Samuel 16:7

# RICH INDEED

*I*t was the famous Patrick Henry who wrote in his will: "This is all the inheritance I can give to my dear family. The religion of Christ will give them one which will make them rich indeed."

Our most precious riches are in the heart, not the purse. If the heart is filled with faith, hope, love, self-respect, peace and good will, that person is rich. The richest rich! Because those means supply the greatest need!

Therefore, while we are laying up some valuables for our physical needs, we should not neglect to put a few in the heart. They count most!

*It is bad to have an empty purse,*
*But an empty heart is a whole lot worse.*
— Nixon Waterman

*There is one who makes himself rich,*
*yet has nothing; and one who makes himself poor,*
*yet has great riches.*
— Proverbs 13:7

# MOST NEVER HAPPENED

*U*nless we watch our imaginations, we are sure to have more troubles than we can handle. We already have enough without entertaining more in fantasy.

A hyperactive imagination creates shadowy dangers and unreal burdens, but they scare and tire and weary us as much as if they were genuine.

It is more practical to be realistic, to see things as they are, no better or worse; for some people have troubles and don't know it, while others have no troubles and think they do.

It was Mark Twain who said, "I am an old man and have known a great many troubles, but most of them never happened."

*Though life is made up of mere bubbles*
*'Tis better than many aver,*
*For while we've a whole lot of troubles*
*The most of them never occur.*
— Nixon Waterman

*Behold, I know your thoughts, and the devices*
*which ye wrongfully imagine against me.*
— Job 21:27

# PICK THE TIME

*D*iscretion is the better part of wisdom— and of valor. Any fool can speak or act at the wrong time. No matter how good a word or deed may be, there are times when it is inappropriate. Even the fox is known for his superior prudence; he picks his time to strike.

The best of talents will fail, if the use of them is not properly timed. After all, even judgment is needed to fly a kite— not every day is a likely time. To know when to act is a whole education wrapped up in one word— discretion.

*Discretion is putting two and two together*
*and keeping our mouth shut.*
— Anonymous

*To everything there is a season,*
*a time for every purpose under heaven. . .*
*a time to keep silence, and a time to speak.*
— Ecclesiastes 3:1-7

*October 26*

# HALF AND HALF RELIGION

Halfway religion is no religion, for religion plus a certain feeling against religion equals nothing. The calling to serve God will not tolerate a lukewarm state that is neither hot nor cold, a little for and a little against. It won't do us any good to reluctantly bow in prayer on mocking knees and mumble platitudes with a forked tongue.

However, giving God undivided devotion is the most sustaining experience in all the world. It will warm and enlarge our hearts for God and others, and give us strength to stand up to any eventuality, come what may.

*Thou hast made us for Thyself, O Lord;*
*and our heart is restless until it rests in Thee.*

— St. Augustine
354-430

*So then, because you are lukewarm,*
*and neither cold nor hot,*
*I will spew you out of My mouth.*

— Revelation 3:16

# JUST SAY THANKS

"*T*thank you" are three very important words. We should learn to speak them. Naturally. Sincerely. No person deserves more than he is thankful for. And the size of one's gratitude is not dependent upon the size of the object or favor received, but rather upon the size of the heart.

Gratefulness is a basic support which keeps life from sagging. It is a necessary quality of greatness and nobility. It is a prerequisite of happiness, for no soul's joy can be deeper than his thankfulness. Furthermore, it is an excellent way to return a gift— just say, "I thank you," for this is a payment to the giver.

*I can no other answer make but thanks,*
*and thanks, and ever thanks.*
— William Shakespeare
1564-1616


*. . .and be thankful.*
— Colossians 3:15

# FACE TO FACE

*T*here are many advantages in coming face to face with the person from whom you have become estranged. It creates a warmth that distance will not generate. It permits a smile to speak a rhetoric that cannot be worded. Personal bigness is tested. Tolerance becomes more tolerant, understanding more understandable.

The little differences between us begin to shrink, because we are in the presence of something bigger, the person himself. Being in his presence affords us the opportunity to see that he really has no horns, no pitchfork, no vindictive glare. It lets us see our grievances in his face, and there we have a better chance to behold his motive and not his act.

*Face to face brings you to the intent,*
*And to how he erred in what he meant.*
— Anonymous

*Come, let us look one another in the face.*
— II Kings 14:8

*October 29*

## A SENSE OF FAMILY

*W*hether we are single, married, with children, without children— we are all part of a family. We all had parents; most of us have brothers and sisters, aunts and uncles.

The family is the one best place in all the world...
- where we can be ourselves— to dream and grow
- where we learn the true meaning of love as commitment not flowery emotion
- where God is honored, His truths are taught, and our spirits are nourished
- where we seek protection from the hurts of others
- where we first learn the basic values that will guide us in our careers and bless our friendships

We each have a lot to be thankful for— even if our parents were not perfect. Our responsibility is to take the good and pass it on to a new generation— children, nieces, nephews, even cousins.

*A happy family is but an earlier heaven.*
— John Bowring
1792-1872

*Go home to your family and tell them how much the Lord has done for you.*
— Mark 5:19

# THE PLACE OF PEACE

 eace of heart depends on the heart— what we are, not where we are. There is no need to look for it beyond the mountains nor over the seas. Neither will we find it in what we possess, but rather in what possesses us.

If we find peace, it will be in our own hearts, hearts big enough to hold what peace is: the melody of love, the calmness of an approving conscience, the serenity of a single faith, the composure of courage, the tranquility of self-acceptance, the repose of unselfishness, the harmony of being in tune with self.

*Peace, heart of mine; no longer sigh to wander,*
*Lose not thy life in fruitless quest.*
*There are no happy islands over yonder;*
*Come home and rest.*
— Henry Van Dyke

*I will both lie down in peace,*
*and sleep.*
— Psalm 4:8

# THE BITTER AND THE SWEET

*B*lessed is the one who sugar-coats the bitter he must swallow. Each one of us must take a certain amount of bitters or famish. For our world is not all sweet.

Reality requires us to take a little of the bad with the good. This is true of a friend— none is faultless. True of a mate— no two people are always in complete accord. True of a job— none is a Paradise. True of a school— all err. True of a church. And while the word "church" stirs a hallowed thought, it is made up of humans who are not yet prepared to don halos.

So we must not pass up the sweets because there are bitters; if there were no bitter, we would not know what sweet was.

*They saw the glory of the world displayed;*
*They saw the bitter of it, and the sweet.*
— Ernest Dowson
1867-1900

*But to a hungry soul*
*every bitter thing is sweet.*
— Proverbs 27:7

# A GOOD NAME

good name is not enough— we ought to merit it. Reputation is what people think we are, or think we are not; but character is what we are. A person can gain a good name by publicly denouncing crime while he privately practices it. Stealing secretly and giving openly will cause the world to applaud, but the doer knows he is a fraud.

When a man was asked how much he treasured his name, he replied, placing his hand over his heart, "Not half as much as what I have right here." He was more concerned with being than with seeming.

*Reputation is what men and women think of us.*
*Character is what God and the angels know of us.*
— Thomas Paine
1737-1809

*You wear a name that says you are alive,*
*but you are dead.*
— Revelation 3:1

*November 2*

## LAUGHTER PROTECTS

When a little boy on his scooter hit a bump in the sidewalk and took a tumble, he paused and then burst out laughing.

A passer-by who saw no fun in the bruises asked: "What's so funny? Why laugh about it?"

The boy replied, "I'm laughing so I won't cry."

Occasionally we adults hit a rough place in life and suffer a spill; now that is a good time to laugh, lest we lose self-possession. Laughing is a safety-valve which lets off the tensions of irritations and promotes health. It is the cheapest medicine and aspirin free. It is better than "new and improved," it is old and it works.

*If you are not allowed to laugh in heaven,*
*I don't want to go there.*
— Martin Luther
1483-1546

*A cheerful, happy heart*
*is good medicine.*
— Proverbs 17:22

*November 3*

# MERCY COMES DOWN

*T*here is no greater badge of nobility than mercy. It is the formation of so many noble traits. Like the rainbow, it sparkles with many colors: clemency, compassion, forgiveness, pity, yearning. It's one of the measurements of a person; our size is in proportion to our compassion.

If experience makes the person, then it makes mercy more merciful. The need of compassion we have felt in ourselves is more easily extended to others. If we have broken a leg, we are more sympathetic toward the one who limps. Just knowing that unrelenting justice would down us all, we should be more inclined toward clemency for other offenders.

*Mercy comes down from heaven to earth*
*so that we by practicing it may resemble God.*
— G. Giraldi

*Blessed are the merciful,*
*for they shall obtain mercy.*
— Matthew 5:7

*November 4*

## ENRICHED BY GIVING

Giving is better really than receiving, though it is contrary to popular belief. Of course, receiving is good; if not, giving is not good, for we can't have one without the other. But of the two, giving is the more rewarding.

Julius Caesar is reputed to have said that no music was as charming to his ears as the requests of his friends, and the supplications of those in want of his assistance.

A giving hand is a gathering hand— it collects more than it hands out. It is most ennobling. It is the life of love. It is humanity's touch of divinity in one word.

*Give! as the morning that flows out of heaven;*
*Give! as the waves when their channel is riven;*
*Give! as the free air and sunshine are given;*
*Lavishly, utterly, joyfully give!*
— Anonymous


*It is more blessed to give than to receive.*
— Acts 20:35

# THE GIVER WITH THE GIFT

*W*ho gives himself, with his gift, gives the most— life to life. All other giving is small.

Gifts! gifts! how we love them! If they come as gifts— not deceits; if they express goodness— not bribes; if they are free acts of thoughtfulness not attached to gain-seeking strings and hidden motives.

If we have a message, we can say it with a gift; and it will keep speaking, unless we prove unkind. Remember— the gift and the giver belong together. They are not good if detached. And so for the highest form of giving, we must remain true long after the gift has vanished.

*What brings joy to the heart*
*is not so much the friend's gift*
*as the friend's love.*
— St. Ailred
1109-1167

*A present is a precious stone in the eyes of its possessor;*
*wherever he turns he prospers.*
— Proverbs 17:8

## NOT SKIN DEEP

The fairest beauty is that which no camera can catch. When beauty is only skin deep, others can see beneath the surface. Outward beauty intoxicates the eye, but inward beauty grabs the heart.

The comeliness which catches the eye can be deceptive, a pretty body with an ugly heart. External handsomeness is the package nature provides, but internal handsomeness is the contents each person develops. Only a few of us can have the former, but there is no excuse for anyone's not having the latter. And as for values, it is a poor product when the container is worth more than the contents.

*Handsome is that handsome does.*
— Oliver Goldsmith
1728-1774

*You...made your beauty to be abhorred.*
— Ezekiel 16:25

# THE ROOT OF
# MUCH ATTENTION

*M*oney does not make one more winsome— just more welcome. For "the love of money is the root of" much attention for those who have it. Health is more valuable than wealth, but the sick rich man gets more invitations. A request for his presence, however, may be only to reach for his purse, and those doors that money opens may slam him on the way out— after his pockets are picked.

Therefore, if we have only thirty coins, watch that Judas kiss— its lips have a taste for silver. And we should not be fooled by a little homage; for where money is god, the servants bow.

> *Prosperity makes friends,*
> *adversity tries them.*
> — Publius Syrus
> First Century B. C.

> *Wealth makes many friends. . .*
> — Proverbs 19:4

# LOVE CHANGES THE LOOKS

*N*othing gives the world a new look like the rose-colored glasses of love. The oceans are bluer, the grass greener, the flowers sweeter, the moon brighter, and even the old grouch down the street seems nicer.

The world has its tragedies and comedies and because of love, its beauty and brotherhood.

Love gives us something sweet when we are threatened with the bitter, a light brighter than the sun when other lights fade, a wealth richer than Solomon when bankruptcy threatens, an ointment for the heart when it has been pierced, a helping hand when we falter.

It is the magic of beauty, the spring of goodness, the bond of closeness.

*Love puts the fun in together, the sad in apart,*
*the hope in tomorrow, the joy in a heart.*
— Anonymous

*But above all these things put on love,*
*which is the bond of perfection.*
— Colossians 3:14

*November 9*

# WISELY SILENT

There are so many instances when well-timed silence is better than speech:

- When we don't know what to say
- When we don't know how to say it
- When others don't care to hear it
- When talking would hurt another
- When we may later regret it
- When slander is to be answered best
- When the heart is so heavy that speech seems light
- When suffering prefers to remain mute
- When saying nothing is the grandest eloquence
- When quietude is most persuasive

Remember— the stars shine in silence, and so can we.

*Let thy speech be better than silence, or be silent.*
— Dionysius the Elder
430-367 B. C.

*But Jesus gave him no answer.*
— John 19:9

## DEVELOP GOOD HABITS

*T*oday is mine provided my habits let me possess it. For habits not only make the day, they make me.

Habit eventually becomes character; for what we do and repeat becomes us— and our days. Spontaneous action for the right makes one an ideal person. Accordingly, our second nature is not second best.

Habits are the avenues through which mankind largely moves, but not every street leads to where we should go. So, we choose with care our destiny, and then through consistent usage, establish a set of habits that will take us on our way.

*The second half of life*
*is made up of the habits*
*we acquired during the first half.*
— Fyodor Dostoyevski
1812-1881

*And as His custom was,*
*He went into the synagogue on the sabbath day.*
— Luke 4:16

# A WOMAN NAMED SUNSHINE

*I* once knew a woman named "Sunshine." Oh, that is not what her mother and father named her at birth. But that's what we— her friends, her spiritual brothers and sisters— called her.

Maybe it was her smile, or her dazzling, radiant eyes, or her impetuous desire to have fun and experience life. Even in old age, she had more spunk than a teenager.

Whatever she had, somehow it got all over the rest of us every time we were with her. That stuff was contagious. I loved it.

> *Those who bring sunshine to the lives of others*
> *cannot keep it from themselves.*
> — James Barrie

> *And he shall be as the light of the morning,*
> *when the sun riseth.*
> — II Samuel 23:4

*November 12*

# HEARTS IN PRAYER

We must put our hearts in prayer, if prayer would put heart in us. Our prayers, whether in public or in private, should be heart-felt expressions to God. We must open our hearts and let the sincerity and simplicity of what's there come forth.

The main thing is not the arithmetic of prayers— how numerous they are; nor the range of prayers— how long they are; nor the linguistics of prayers— how grammatical they are; nor the rhetoric of prayers— how eloquent they are; nor the music of prayers— how sweet the voice is; nor the posture of prayers— how the body poses. The chief part of prayer is the heart. Do we have a heart for God?

*Pray as you can,*
*for prayer doesn't consist of thinking a great deal,*
*but loving a great deal.*
— Theresa of Avila
1515-1582

*I call with all my heart; answer me,*
*O Lord, and I will obey your decrees.*
— Psalm 119:145

# CLIMBING THE LADDER

All of us have been encouraged to climb the ladder of success— at work, in social circles, in political organizations, and even a few in church hierarchies.

Climbing is good. Advancement is to be achieved. But maybe a few caution signs are in order before we continue the journey:

*He that never climbed never fell.*
— John Heywood

*The most difficult part of climbing the ladder is getting through the crowd at the bottom.*
— Roger Babson

*Before starting to climb the ladder of success, be sure the ladder is not against the wrong wall.*
— Anonymous

*Seek ye first the kingdom of God.*
— Mathew 6:33

*November 14*

# BETTER TRUST ALL THAN NONE

We may lose occasionally in trusting too many, but we will lose more in trusting too few. For the workings of society are but a trust, without which we won't fit in.

While a few people will prove false, the majority will compensate. There is more to gain in standing with those who are so good they think no one is bad, than to stand with those who are so bad they think no one is good. The wiser practice, however, is to be discriminatory with a leaning toward trust.

Suspicion is a boomerang that will later come back to maim us. When we are suspicious of everyone, everyone will soon be suspicious of us.

*To be trusted is a greater compliment*
*than to be loved.*
— George Macdonald
1824-905

*And Achish believed David.*
— I Samuel 27:12

*November 15*

## TIED TO SELF

What do I get out of it? That is the question coming from the self-centered person. Want the answer? Not much! The reason— it will keep one from giving much, and in return the world will reciprocate sparingly. No one can get much from self-centeredness, for it is littleness— a big interest in a little object.

We can't go far, if we are tied to self. Self-absorption forges the chains which bind us to our own unhappiness, cynicism and defeat. And that we are left bound— but not gagged— while the world passes us by.

*If you wish to be miserable, think much about yourself;*
*about what you want, what you like, what respect people*
*ought to pay you, and what people think of you.*
— Charles Kingsley

*. . .not seeking my own profit,*
*but the profit of many. . .*
— I Corinthians 10:33

## TOO GOOD A BARGAIN

*I* learned one of the most useful lessons of my life when I was a child— to be cautious of unreasonable bargains. I bought some apples at a greatly reduced price. They looked good, but what I didn't see was the rotten ones on the bottom. I was swindled by the hope of getting something for nothing. Having been relieved of my little cash, I resolved that if I had more sense than a green apple I would from that day proceed in life with more inspection.

Nothing worthwhile in business, education, politics or religion comes free. About all we get free is fresh air and doubtful advice.

*You get what you pay for.*
— Gabriel Biel
1425-1495

*The king's merchants received*
*the linen yarn at a price.*
— I Kings 10:28

*November 17*

# WHERE HONOR LIES

An old English farmer, leaving his sons a small inheritance, wrote in his will: "There is not a dishonest shilling in the whole of it." All had come through honest toil and honest dealings. He was a man of honor inside and out. His integrity had given him more joy than his wealth.

Nothing in life will bring us much genuine satisfaction unless we keep our honor and self-respect.

It was in this vein that James A. Garfield said: "There is one man whose respect I must have at all hazards, and his name is James A. Garfield, for I must room with him, walk with him, work with him, eat with him, commune with him— live with him."

*It is a worthier thing to deserve honor than to possess it.*
— Anonymous

*A gracious woman retains honor.*
— Proverbs 11:16

# HOW TO HAVE A MINT

*I*t is exceedingly wise to live within our incomes. Economy gives an independence not afforded otherwise. One way to have a mint is to practice thrift, for a dollar saved is a dollar made. It is much harder to spend money discretely than to earn it; and harder still to leave some unspent. "Live within your means" is a good motto; but still a better one is, "Save something today, for it may rain tomorrow."

While it is true that there will be no pockets in our shroud, it is just as true that it will take somebody's money to buy one.

*Economy has frequently nothing whatever to do*
*with the amount of money being spent,*
*but with the wisdom used in spending it.*
— Henry Ford

*For which of you, intending to build a tower,*
*does not sit down first and count the cost,*
*whether he has enough to finish it?*
— Luke 14:28

# TO BE A CANDLE

It is gratifying to be a candle. Human beams shine far, and if they shine far, they shine near. The darker the night, the brighter they shine, though quietly. We must not mistake the silence of light; it is effective without noise. A candle blows no horn, it just shines.

As no one knows where light goes when it goes out, no one knows a good deed's whereabouts except that it does not end. This is one way we can be immortal— we can just be a light.

*I don't have to light all the world,*
*but I do have to light my part.*
— Anonymous

*You, O Lord, keep my lamp burning;*
*my God turns my darkness into light.*
— Psalm 18:28

# GOD'S UNIVERSITY

*T*he four years (or more) spent in university life may have been enjoyable, satisfying and memorable, but they were not intended to accomplish that alone.

We were not there to just make friends, make waves, and make memories. We were there to prepare ourselves for useful service in a career, to train our minds to think clearly, to civilize ourselves so as to be good members of society.

God's University is much the same— we call it life. In it we prepare ourselves for the next plateau, for useful service, for a good long visit with God and His people. Oh, if we don't want to go, God will not force us. We have a choice. But if we plan to spend a lot of time with Him in the future, maybe we should get to know Him a little better now.

*My great concern is not whether God is on my side,*
*my great concern is to be on God's side.*
— Abraham Lincoln

*The heavens declare the glory of God*
*and the firmament proves his handywork.*
— Psalm 19:1

# UPS AND DOWNS

*L*ife is uneven. It has its ups and downs. There are days of exaltation and there are days of despair. The weather is mixed with sunshine and shadow. Some days are too short, others too long. There are valleys to traverse and mountains to climb. Sailing some seas is smooth, others choppy.

But in spite of all this, it is a good day when we can crawl out of bed, put on our clothes, make an honest living, eat a good meal and be a friend to others. God told us life would be like this. After all this is not heaven.

*There is nothing in this world. Today we are on top, tomorrow we are at the bottom of the ladder.*
— Denis Diderot
1713-1784

*For lo, the winter is past, the rain is over and gone. The flowers appear on the earth.*
— Song of Solomon 2:11, 12

# TO CORRECT IS HUMAN

*I*f "to err is human," then to correct is also human. God has no need to make amends, for He errs not. However, as a human it is no disgrace to be what we are: fallible people. But as a maker of mistakes, we should also be a corrector of them. Error accompanies the struggles of mankind, and redressing them is the struggle of our improvement.

If there is anything that needs correcting, do it; seek pardon; close a breach; make retribution. If our blunders cannot be redressed, at least we can make it right with God and ourselves, and then we should forget it.

*I have never met a man who has given me*
*as much trouble as myself.*
— Dwight L. Moody

*If fire breaks out and catches in thorns, so that stacked*
*grain, standing grain, or the field is consumed,*
*he who kindled the fire shall surely make restitution.*
— Exodus 22:6

# TWO OF A KIND

Which is worse? A slanderous tongue or slanderous ears? Since like tongue is welcome only in like ears, then why ask which is worse: the wicked guest or the wicked host?

Stealing another's reputation is not a job for a lone robber. The name-snatcher has to have help in this most despicable thievery, which robs the victim without enriching the spoilers. The vicious tongue wags in vain unless there are defaming ears to listen, and vice versa.

> *Who steals my purse steals trash;*
> *'tis something, nothing;*
> *'Twas mine, 'tis his,*
> *and has been slave to thousands;*
> *But he that filches from me my good name*
> *Robs me of that which not enriches him,*
> *And makes me poor indeed.*
> — William Shakespeare
> 1564-1616

> *Those who seek to hurt me speak of destruction,*
> *and plan deceit all the day long.*
> — Psalm 38:12

## ALTARS ALTER

*T*his is not just a nice pun for wordsmiths to ponder. The altars we erect, the gods we worship on those altars, will alter us forever. We are fashioned and changed by what we love and who we worship.

We're not talking lip service worship, we are talking about the real thing. What or who in our lives are we really devoted to, seek at all costs, have our hearts fully tuned to?

If it is God, we have hope. If it is not God, we need to stop and rethink some things.

*The instinct to worship is hardly less strong
than the instinct to eat.*

— Dorothy Thompson

*Worship the Lord thy God
and him only shalt thou serve.*

— Matthew 4:10

*November 25*

# ALL HAVE SOME

*E*very person has many blessings and at least a few misfortunes. The ones we reflect upon will either strengthen or weaken us.

Our most necessary blessings are apt to be uncounted, because they are the most common: sunshine, rain, oxygen, soil, plants, animals, and a thousand other workings of nature.

The universality of so many blessings, however, does not lower their value. If this commonness tempts us to be ungrateful, let us ask: Where would we stand if the earth caved in? What would we breathe if the oxygen ran out? What would we do if the water dried up?

*Reflect upon your present blessings,*
*of which every man has many—*
*not on your past misfortunes,*
*of which all men have some.*
— Charles Dickens
1812-1870

*Every good thing we have is from above,*
*and comes down from the Father of lights.*
— James 1:17

# TRUST STRENGTHENS US

*T*rust is a quality of life which makes today mine. If I doubt, I lose it.

It is better to have no food in the house than no trust in the heart. Empty living is often due to a lack of expectancy. Some people work and pray (at least they call it prayer), but don't expect very much.

The food will digest better today, if we trust God for more tomorrow. Floods, droughts, pestilences, but mankind survives; so obviously it's not impractical to trust.

And more importantly than just physical things, we can trust God to provide emotional healing, spiritual nourishment and Divine direction.

> *On God for all events depend;*
> *You cannot want when God's your friend.*
> *Weigh well your part and do your best;*
> *Leave to your Maker all the rest.*
>
> — Nathaniel Cotton
> 1705-1788

> *You prepare a table before me in the presence of my enemies;*
> *You anoint my head with oil;*
> *my cup runs over.*
>
> — Psalm 23:5

# DOES MY FAITH LOOK UP?

*F*aith in God strengthens. As a young American preacher, Ray Palmer, sat in his little room meditating on his problems. Suddenly, impulsively he began to write, "My Faith Looks Up to Thee." Quickly, he finished the hymn which has inspired millions.

A few years later Dr. Lowell Mason, the great song writer, requested Palmer to contribute a song to a book he was publishing. Palmer remembered this one and presented it to Mason for publication.

Subsequently, the two men met again. "Mr. Palmer," said Mason, "you may live a long time and you may do many great things, but you will be known forever as the man who wrote "My Faith Looks Up to Thee."

*My faith looks up to thee,*
*Thou Lamb of Calvary,*
*Savior Divine*
*Now hear me while I pray;*
*Take all my guilt away;*
*O let me from this day be wholly Thine.*

— Ray Palmer
written 1830

*And this is the victory that has overcome*
*the world— our faith.*

— I John 5:4

*November 28*

# NO WHERE TO GO

*M*any times we cannot get the courage to stand on our feet until we get on our knees. In addition to the Divine assistance, prayer helps us gather our inner resources which afford strength.

It is in this sacred experience that we, stripped of deceit and vanity (for there is no point in trying to fool ourselves or God), may honestly discuss and earnestly petition God's help for our frailties and faults, trials and troubles, aims and ambitions.

A pouring out of the deepest and truest feelings, a communication of spirit with Spirit, that is what it is. And that is praying.

*I have been driven many times to my knees*
*by the overwhelming conviction*
*that I had no where else to go.*
— Abraham Lincoln

*We always should pray*
*and not lose heart.*
— Luke 18:1

*November 29*

# A THREAD OF LOVE

*N*o rope or cable on earth can bind as fast as a single thread of love. It fastens like a lock and is stronger than steel. None of us can know its true power unless we have been on one end of the strand. It is too strong for any mortal to describe— except in one word: God, for "God is Love."

It is the golden thread which binds heart to heart: the irresistible, unseen force that draws us together, you to me and me to you. It is the world's most unifying quality, which makes each a part of all.

*The sweetest lives are those to duty wed,*
*Whose deeds both great and small,*
*Are close knit strands of an unbroken thread,*
*Where love ennobles all.*

— Anonymous

*That their hearts might be encouraged,*
*being knit together in love, and attaining to all riches*
*of the full assurance of understanding.*

— Colossians 2:2

# PROTECTED BY SELF-RESPECT

There is one person whose approval is worth more than all others. That one is me! As long as I keep his or her respect, the ill reports of others can't permanently hurt me; but lose it, and all the good that may be said of me is of little help.

What we think of ourselves is most important. There is great strength in remaining pure and maintaining self-respect. It will clothe us with an armor our detractors cannot pierce. If we are ever hurt deep down inside, beneath the skin, we will have to do it.

*None but one can harm you,*
*None but yourself who are your greatest foe;*
*He that respects himself is safe from others,*
*He wears a coat of mail that none can pierce.*
— Henry Wadsworth Longfellow
— 1807-1882

*The righteous will hold to his way, and he who has*
*clean hands will be stronger and stronger.*
— Job 17:9

# I HEAR THE WHISPERS

We cannot postpone living. Don't let life pass us by while we only endure the present. Don't wait for the children to grow up— have a good time while they do. Don't wait until we get that new house— a new outlook is more urgent. Don't wait until all the debts are paid— we might have more later. Don't wait for retirement— then we might be tired.

Those who wait to enjoy life may find it a little late. Every day has a parade of puny problems come begging us to delay the joy. They whisper, "Tomorrow." But God whispers, "Today."

*He who neglects the present moment*
*throws away all he has.*
— Johann von Schiller
1759-1805

*Encourage one another daily, while it is called Today.*
— Hebrews 3:13

*December 2*

# THE DECISION TO DECIDE

*M*ake decisions, make them as wisely as we can, but make them. The fate of life begins with choice, and it is our fate and our prerogative to call the turns that determine it.

Those who will not decide have already decided— against success and happiness. It is better to make some bad decisions than to continuously make the worst one of all— no decision.

Weigh the pros and cons. Get all the expert help we can, but reserve the right to decide. Standing up to life is like being a patient when the doctors disagree; you have to make the final judgment.

*When you have to make a choice*
*and don't make it, that is in itself a choice.*
— William James

*So shall your judgment be;*
*you yourself have made the decision.*
— I Kings 20:40

## December 3

# WHEN SOMEBODY IS ME

*It* is easy to say, "Somebody ought to do that." I have a nice list of all the things somebody should do. But maybe that somebody is me! My being smart enough to see what should be done is a mighty good sign that I'm big enough to do it.

I should take the initiative. It won't do any good to visualize an oak unless I plant an acorn. I must take action. Move. Nevertheless, I should be deliberate, not "rush in where angels dare to tread." But where angels lead, I should walk in with my eyes open and my sleeves rolled up.

Vision, action, accomplishment, this is the pattern of fortune.

*Take time to deliberate;*
*but when the time for action arrives,*
*stop thinking and go in.*
— Andrew Jackson

*Then I said, "Here am I! Send me."*
— Isaiah 6:8

*December 4*

# LINKED TO OTHERS

One of our supreme needs is a link with others. We crave the closeness and happiness of association. We find assistance in wholesome companions. They can bear our sorrow and share our joys. They can steady us when we wobble. They can lift us up when we fall. They can sit beside us when we are sick. They can play with us when we are well.

We all want this bond of helpfulness. The method of obtaining it is simple— love people. Love will fasten us to the other end of the link.


*Love alone is capable of uniting living beings in such a way as to complete and fulfill them, for it alone takes them and joins them by what is deepest in themselves.*

— Pierre Teilhard de Chardin


*The soul of Jonathan was knit to the soul of David, and Jonathan loved him as his own soul.*

— I Samuel 18:1

# A FRIEND OF TRUTH

*T*here is no future in fighting truth. We can't win. What sometimes is judged victory is premature. Truth won't fall dead in the streets; what appears to be its corpse is only its wounded form dragged into an alley; but look— there it comes again, as straight and strong and unconquerable as ever. No need to try to bury it, for it has inherent resurrection powers and shall rise again.

But of course no sane person wants to fight truth. The lesson for us is to not give up the truth even when we see evil and falsehood seeming to prevail. The victory is only temporary, only apparent and most definitely hollow.

*The greatest friend of truth is Time, her greatest enemy is Prejudice, and her constant companion is Humility.*
— Charles Colton

*I have chosen to follow the way of truth.*
— Psalm 119:30

*December 6*

# A CUP OF KINDNESS

All of us have heard of "a cup of kindness," but I have seen it. And so have you.

I even see it in a real cup, as when my wife pours tea or coffee. Most of the time we see it in so many varied forms we seldom take note.

Kindness cannot be commanded, or bought, or stolen, or even hidden for long. Kindness is brewed and steeped in humble hearts and flows out quietly, gently like tea from a teapot. And the best part— the more of it we serve to others, the more we have left.

*I wonder why we are not all kinder to each other than we are. How much the world needs it! How easily it is done.*

— Henry Drummond

*Holy and beloved, put on the clothes of kindness...*
— Colossians 3:1

# ONE GRAVE OR TWO?

*R*evenge is supposed to be sweet, at least it is in the movies. The hurt and wounded person gets a knife, a gun or a vicious tongue and goes looking for the assailant. And most of us cheer him or her on.

But in reality, most of us are not attacked by thugs or criminals or white collar cheats. We all receive our share of insults, hurts and slight offenses.

The question is: when we are wronged, are we going to be forgiving or forever savages? Are we going to outgrow our need for revenge and thus break the cycle of perpetual strife? Like most things, somebody has to start it, somebody has to be big enough to appear little.

*He who seeks revenge digs two graves.*
— Ancient Proverb

*Whoever digs a pit for others will fall into it himself.*
— Proverbs 26:27

*December 8*

# TWO SIDES
# ARE BETTER THAN ONE

*D*on't you think we should hear the other side? It just might be possible that we heard the wrong report. If we listened to only one version, we may not have heard the whole story, the whole truth. If we consider all the facts, impartially, we might be tempted to take the other side.

The trouble is, it requires less effort to be hasty than correct. And it is easier to take sides, right or wrong, where our personal sympathies lie. But one truth is crystal clear: judgments should never be formed on either half facts or personal preferences.

*This world belongs to the person who is wise enough to change his mind in the presence of the facts.*
— Ray L. Smith

*Wisdom is found in doing what is right and just and fair.*
— Proverbs 1:2,3

# THEY ALWAYS COME BACK

Be slow about marking people off your list. Mercy in our own heart makes the wounds more tolerable. There is too much good in the worst of the worst and too much bad in the best of the best for us to be unforgiving.

If we are mistreated, we can rise above it. If others condemn us, we can be magnanimous. If others are little, we can be big. If there is a tug-of-war, we can let our end of the rope be charity.

Remember, the cat and the kindness we give away always come back to us. We win by acting bigger than little people.

*Better to do a kindness near at home*
*than walk a thousand miles to burn incense.*
— Ancient Proverb

*Though I speak with the tongues of men and of angels,*
*but have not love, I am become as sounding brass,*
*or a clanging cymbal.*
— I Corinthians 13:1

*December 10*

# SEEK PEACE

*P*eace is positive. Something to seek. And when it is sought, it is apt to be found, for most people respond in the manner we treat them.

Peace is the tolerance of faults, the willingness to give a little, the triumph of principles, the unselfish pursuit of right which is stronger than might.

The peacemaker has a reconstructed view of life which puts the time and talent of conflict to a better cause. He does more than put up the sword— he beats it into a plowshare. He does more than lay aside the spear— he forges it into a pruning hook. He overcomes evil with good.

*Peace, like every other rare and precious thing, doesn't come to us. We have to go and get it.*
— Faith Forsythe

*Pursue peace with all men.*
— Hebrews 12:14

*December 11*

# MANNERS MATTER

*G*ood manners and good sense go together. Uncivility reflects on our thinking. If like manners produce like reactions, then the impolite person sorely has not thought through the consequences of his poor behavior.

Good manners will make us welcome, for they put people at ease, allowing others to see our good will. It is the civilized way of doing things— not like the primitive way of animals. Courtesy is the refinement which makes human relations run smoothly, without which there is friction.

One thing we can do, even if we are bankrupt, is to be civil; though it costs nothing, it is friends in hand and food on the table.


*The small courtesies sweeten life:*
*the greater ennoble it.*
— Bovée


*And Julius courteously entreated Paul.*
— Acts 27:3

*December 12*

# MIND OUR OWN BUSINESS

One way to be successful and happy is to mind our own business— not another's. A basic human right is that our personal affairs be inviolate, unless we are infringing on the rights of others.

Solomon says that meddling is as unhelpful and dangerous as taking a dog by the ears— we don't help the dog, and we may get bitten. Furthermore, the meddlers I know are not well qualified. Most of the people that are passing out the free advice and meddling are the ones who have the most problems of their own.

Therefore, we have enough matters of our own to tend to before we try to solve other people's problems. Let others keep their problems so that we can keep our friends.

*To be idle is a curse,*
*But to be a busybody is a whole lot worse.*
— Anonymous

*But let none of you suffer. . . as a busybody*
*in other people's matters.*
— I Peter 4:15

*December 13*

# GIVE IT A REST

*I*t's a pity to get on a topic and can't get off. Harping on the same string is an imposition on another person's time and ears. The identical tune gets monotonous, and in time will vex the most patient listener. There is no quicker way to cause the welcome mat to shrink. The squeak of the hinges on the person's door as you exit is sweeter to him than your one-string harping.

Enough is enough! Give it a rest! And the kindest thing we can say about the harper is that he possesses a plentiful lack of good judgment. So that others will enjoy us, we must learn to play more than one tune.

*Harp so on the same string.*
— Miguel De Cervantes
1547-1616

*A continual dripping on a very rainy day*
*and a contentious woman or man are alike.*
— Proverbs 27:15

# PAIN IN THE PLAN

*P*ain! pain! how you visit us mortals! And why? That's the question heard from a million voices around the globe. Why? Why? For the ache of mankind grants no exemptions, only some forms and sources of it. Sooner or later it strikes us all.

So— evidently there are some purposes for suffering in the wise plan of the Gracious Designer; for instance: a motivation for action, a teacher of character, a giver of wider dimensions, and a developer of sympathy. Besides, pain reminds us that earth is not Heaven, that Heaven has no suffering, and that God stands ready even now.

*It is by those who have suffered
that the world has been advanced.*

— Leo Tolstoy

*For I reckon that the sufferings of this present time are
not worthy to be compared with the glory which shall be
revealed in us.*

— Romans 8:18

*December 15*

# LOYALTY BEGINS AT HOME

The first requirement of loyalty to others is loyalty to self. The person who is willing to ream himself out to suit everybody cuts away until there is nothing left but an empty shell.

All of us know such make-believe people. And just as a fountain cannot flow from nothing, neither can fidelity spring from a void; that which bubbles forth is only pretension.

The true-to-self person is out-and-out honest, truthful, trustworthy, sincere and constant. Where these attributes prevail, no one need fear betrayal; for it would be like tearing off an arm, the pulling away a part of self.

> *This above all: to thine own self be true,*
> *And it must follow, as the night the day,*
> *Thou canst not then be false to any man.*
>
> — William Shakespeare
> 1564-1616

> *I gave my brother Hanani. . . charge over Jerusalem:*
> *for he was a faithful man. . .*
> — Nehemiah 7:2

# CAN'T COUNT AGE BY YEARS

The young in heart. This phrase has fallen upon our ears for years, long enough to make us either old or young: old if we count birthdays; young if we count feelings. This is true because age defies chronology.

If we would count age, then go to the mind and there use the gauges. Measure the dreams, hopes and ambitions. If these qualities are there in abundance, so is our youth— the dawn of renewed quests with the dawn of each new day— though the years be many.

Age does not count as long as there is something else to count.

*Thou shalt not rob me, thievish Time,*
*Of all my blessings or my joy;*
*I have some jewels in my heart*
*Which thou art powerless to destroy.*
— Charles Mackay
1814-1889

*Though our outward bodies are declining, our inward selves*
*are being renewed day by day.*
— II Corinthians 4:16

*December 17*

# THE SECOND WRONG

It is better to leave an offender to the condemnation of his own conscience than to take vengeance. Fighting him may only make him feel better by giving him a sense of justification. It is more effective to let the pain spring from his own bosom than for us to hurt him.

By refusing to retaliate, we can stay free of offense and save our own heart from a dagger of guilt. Then we can sleep better, work better, play better and pray better. The second wrong never rights the first one, just adds another injury to a world already groaning in guilt.

Besides, we need to let God handle his own business.

*The person who tries to get even by making others suffer for their sins is interfering in God's business.*
— Anonymous

*Vengeance is mine; I will repay says the Lord.*
— Romans 12:19

*December 18*

# THE BEST RULERSHIP

*S*elf-control is the most essential and accomplished form of rulership. Every person's mind can be a throne. And there we can reign, and there we ought to reign.

However, it is a big job, too big for little people. Only the giants in determination can be king of self. Small-minded people abdicate in favor of people, things and circumstances.

The power of our self-preservation is found in our self-control. Those who lose it become helpless, passive creatures with no means of protection. They are as vulnerable as an ancient city with broken down walls.

*He who reigns within himself,*
*and rules passions, desires, and fears,*
*is more than a king.*
— John Milton
1608-1674

*Whoever has no rule over his own spirit*
*is like a city broken down, without walls.*
— Proverbs 25:28

## December 19

# THE FURY OF JEALOUSY

*T*ame jealousy and we will protect ourselves from a deadly fury; from the misery which knows no peace; from the suspicion which suspects and suspects and suspects; from the provocation which creates its own strife; from the vengeance which never spares itself; from a cruelty as cold as the grave; from the fear of losing, which drives away what it would keep; and, worst of all, from the affliction which seems never to end.

If we are still tempted to engage in a little jealousy, we should remember that it will destroy us long before we destroy the object of our venom.

*The venom clamours of a jealous woman*
*Poison more deadly than a mad dog's tooth.*
— William Shakespeare
1564-1616

*For jealousy is the rage of a man;*
*therefore he will not spare in the day of vengeance.*
— Proverbs 6:34

# THE RICHES OF CONTENTMENT

*C*ontentment is the most satisfying riches this poor, troubled world has ever known, richer than any monarch's golden crown.

Contentment is easier to find, if we keep in mind the best things are the nearest: pulse in our veins, sight in our eyes, hearing in our ears, food in our stomach, flowers in our yard, water in our well, employment for our mind and hands, friends in our heart, and the path of God for our feet.

Life's plain, common things provide peace, joy and sleep; and if they do not, neither would the state, position or riches one wishes for.

*My crown is in my heart, not on my head;*
*Not decked with diamonds and Indian Stones,*
*Nor to be seen. My crown is called content.*
*A crown it is that seldom kings enjoy.*
— William Shakespeare
1564-1616

*But godliness with contentment*
*is great gain.*
— I Timothy 6:6

# THE EDUCATION OF FOLLY

*A*t times, all of us have played the fool, but there is a difference: wise fools and stupid fools. The sagacious fool learns from his folly; the thickheaded fool never does. If we can avoid the same blunder, there is hope for us. After all, the world doesn't like the one who never makes a mistake; neither is it fond of the person who keeps on committing the same ones.

Let us take courage: get up from every fall, wipe off the dust and be thankful— not for the slip, not for the bruises, but that we are now a little smarter.

*Folly in all of every age we see,*
*The only difference lies in the degree.*
— Nicholas Boileau-Despreaux
1636-1711

*I have played the fool and erred*
*exceedingly.*
— I Samuel 26:21

# THE BOOK OUR MOTHERS READ

The Bible contains the richest and rarest literature of the world. It appeals to the intellectual and aesthetic as well as to the spiritual and moral faculties. It marks the literature of the scholar just like it colors the speech of the street.

John Ruskin considered the Bible "the grandest group of writings extant in the rational world."

The most brilliant passages of Macaulay's writings are rounded with Scripture quotations.

Pope saturated his classics with quotations from Isaiah.

Cowper's "Task" drew much of its imagery from the Scriptures.

Bryant's "Thanatopsis" could never have been written but for the pages of Job.

And myriads of other authors would never have done so excellently without the Bible.

*And, weary seekers of the best,*
*We come back laden from our quest*
*To find that all the sages said*
*Is in the Book our mothers read.*
— John Greenleaf Whittier
1807-1892

*All scripture is given by inspiration of God*
*and is useful for...*
— II Timothy 3:16

*December 23*

# JESUS CHRIST

*W*hile many people may differ on many points about Jesus Christ, they are agreed that his fame has no rival, that his grip on human hearts has no equal, that his word is sharper than any sword, and that his power to command is mightier than any general.

To his follower, Christ is "the way, the truth, and the life," the Paragon of Goodness, the Model of Morality, and the Savior of the Lost. After nineteen centuries his footprints still glow with a radiant helpfulness, and all who are guided by them lift their own feet of clay to victories over self.

*I ask them whence their victory came:*
*They, with united breath,*
*Ascribe their conquest to the Lamb*
*Their triumph to his death.*
— Isaac Watts
1674-1748

*Christ also suffered for us,*
*leaving us an example,*
*that we should follow his steps.*
— I Peter 2:21

# MORE THAN A MERE MAN

We admire the heroism of Napoleon, the dauntlessness of Caesar, the fortitude of Stonewall Jackson. But would a person call for a Napoleon when his mate lies a corpse, or seek the consolation of a Caesar when he buries his child, or send for a Jackson as he prays at the dying bedside of his mother? No! In these moments we feel the need of a man possessed with more than courage. He craves the aid of a man of sympathy and kindness, a man acquainted with grief, a man whose words can heal a heart that aches and breaks— a man like Jesus!

*Alexander, Caesar, Charlemagne and I myself*
*have founded empires; but upon what do these creations*
*of our genius depend? Upon force. Jesus alone founded*
*His empire upon love, and to this very day*
*millions would die for him.*

— Napoleon Bonaparte
1769-1821

*A man of sorrows and acquainted with grief.*
— Isaiah 53:3

*December 25*

# ANNO DOMINI

*A.D.*— "in the year of our Lord." And while we know not the day he was born, we know he was. How great the influence of that lowly carpenter. So much that men began to reckon time by his coming, and now no one can date a letter without acknowledging his birth.

Yet he never did the things which ordinarily accompany renown, like go to college, write a book, lead a military force, head a government; but he is recognized as the Master Teacher, author of the New Testament, Commander of the mightiest army, King of kings; and though he was the object of strife, he is celebrated as the Prince of Peace.

*The sages and heroes of history are receding from us,*
*and history contracts the record of their deeds*
*into a narrower page. But time has no power*
*over the name and deeds and words of Jesus Christ.*
— William Ellery Channing

*For unto us a child is born. . .*
*and his name shall be called Wonderful, Counselor,*
*The Mighty God, The Everlasting Father,*
*The Prince of Peace.*
— Isaiah 9:6

*December 26*

## DEEPER WELLS

*T*he wellspring of success is found in our hearts. The lessons of biography clearly teach that the greats of history had internal resources from which they drew as they faced their times.

In letting down our buckets and pulling them up, what do we get? Sparkling, fresh, life-renewing strength? Or empty buckets from wells that are dry? When we need extra faith, more courage, stiller calmness, additional self-approval, more generosity, surer steadfastness, and cast down the bucket, do we get the renewal to carry on? Or do we just get older drawing up nothing?

If we want real spiritual nourishment, we need to dig a little deeper.

*. . .dropping buckets into empty wells*
*And growing old in drawing up nothing.*
— William Cowper
1731-1800

*Hold on to the deep truths of the faith.*
— I Timothy 3:9

*December 27*

# GET RIGHT, DO RIGHT

*R*ight is not something just to verbalize on; it is something to be and do. And the steps are simple: know right, believe right and do right. This will give us the basis to hope for attainment, because it is always linked with right.

None of us should expect success unless we are right, for it cannot come from wrong; if it does, it is not success—only disguised failure. As poison is not the makings of a cake, neither are bitter attitudes the ingredients of a sweet life. No wrong road leads to the right place.

Consequently, if wrong, get right; if right, stay right.

*If I am right, Thy grace impart,*
*Still in the right to stay;*
*If I am wrong; O teach my heart*
*To find the better way.*
— Alexander Pope
1688-1744


*For thou has done right. . .*
— Nehemiah 9:33

# TIME, THE BETTER JUDGE

Who succeeds? Not every one who makes history. Many historic characters have failed. Success is not a throne to sit on; it is ruling over self. That gives us our kingdom.

Time passes a better judgment on success than the present. Time has a way of lowering the exalted and exalting the lowered. Nineteen centuries ago the Roman Emperor Nero beheaded the Apostle Paul. Nero did the worst he could and was hailed a success; Paul did the best he could and was scorned a failure. But look at them now. Nero lives in infamy. Paul lives in glory.

*On earth we have nothing to do with success or results,*
*but only with being true to God and for God.*
*Defeat in doing the right is nevertheless victory.*
— F. W. Robertson

*And also if anyone competes in athletics,*
*he is not crowned unless he competes*
*according to the rules.*
— II Timothy 2:5

*December 29*

# NO TURNING BACK

*O*n and *On* are the success twins. They deserve greatness, for there is no greater ability than stability—steadiness in pursuits.

Nothing is impossible to people of constant purpose. In every aspect of life, perseverance rules. Pressing on solves our problems, while turning back brings on more. It's the one who presses on that pushes past the crowd. He finds success where drop-outs find failure. The secret is in a disciplined mind and a strong will that won't give up.

> *We conquer*
> *— not in any brilliant fashion*
> *— we conquer by continuing.*
> — George Matheson

*No one having put his hand to the plow, and looking back,*
*is fit for the kingdom of God.*
— Luke 9:62

# A BLAZE OF VICTORY

*W*inning life's game depends on the closing moments. We have to play it well to the conclusion. Nobody wins by running up a high score at first, then failing in the end. It's the last period that determines the score, and the chief importance of the first ones are their bearing on the last. Don't think we have won just because we are ahead at the half.

It is good to start well, but that is not enough. We must go out in a blaze of victory. It's the way we play at the end that counts.

*Let no one till his death*
*Be called unhappy. Measure not the work*
*Until the day's out and the labor done:*
*Then bring your gauges.*
— Elizabeth Barrett Browning
1806-1861

*I have fought a good fight, I have finished my*
*course, I have kept the faith.*
— II Timothy 4:7

*December 31*

## MY FUTURE

What does the future hold? Much of the past, for history has a way of repeating itself. We handled the past and we can do even better in the future, for hindsight can give us a little foresight, not specifically but generally.

The best thing about the future is that it comes upon us by degrees, a day at a time. We can manage that much.

Whatever it holds, my future is mine: if it be fair weather, let me bask in the sun; if it be storms, let me bend with the wind.

The future belongs to those who can make adjustments and who are willing to work with God as partners for a better life.

*My past is gone; my present is passing;*
*my future is arriving.*
— Anonymous

*Sanctify yourselves for tomorrow.*
— Numbers 11:18

# NOTES

# NOTES

# NOTES

# NOTES

# NOTES

# NOTES

# NOTES

# NOTES

# NOTES

# NOTES

# NOTES